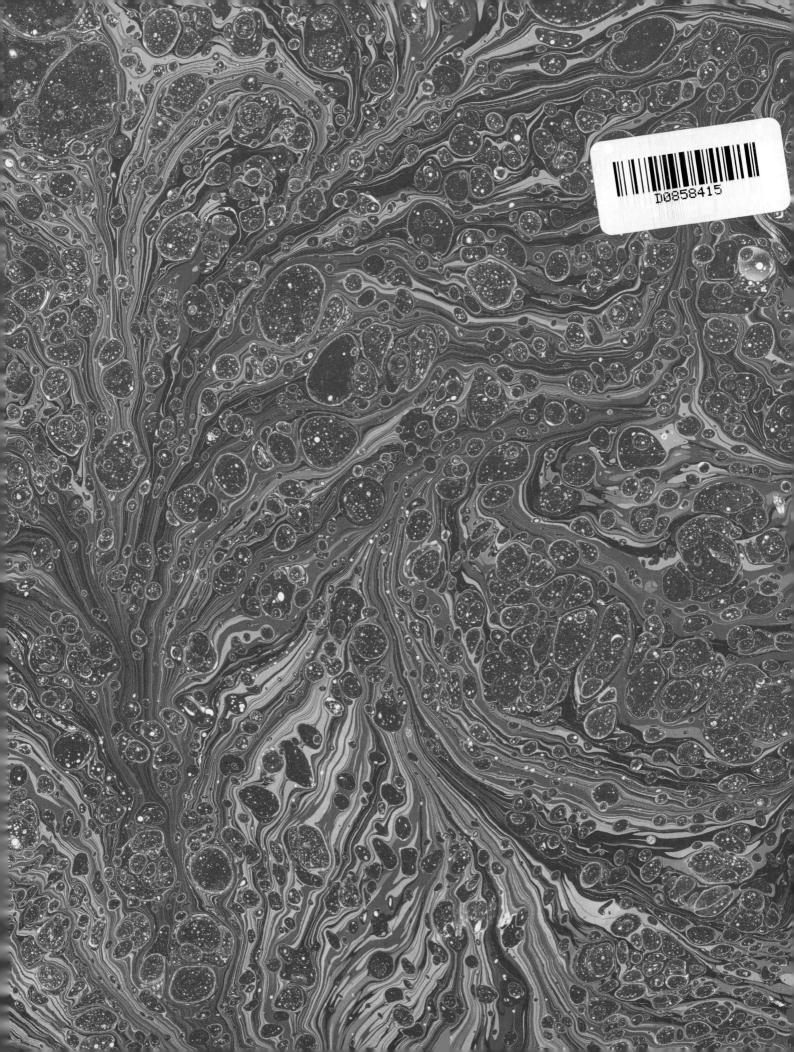

THE CURTISS HYDROAEROPLANE

THE CURTISS HYDROAEROPLANE

THE U.S. NAVY's FIRST AIRPLANE • 1911-1916

Bob Woodling & Taras Chayka

Schiffer Military History
Atglen, PA

Acknowledgments

We are deeply indebted to a great many people who helped us make this book a reality, not the least of whom are our wives, who helped us review our manuscript and who spent many long hours by themselves while we were toiling in isolation. Nor can we ignore the value of the contributions of many other authors, without whose histories of naval aviation we could not have written this book.

Special thanks are due to the many people in the museums and archives of the world who cheerfully supported us by opening their photographic and written materials for us to study. A short list follows: Rick Leisenring, Glenn H. Curtiss Museum; Ed Finney and Chuck Haberlein, Naval Historical Center Photo Section; Gennady Petrov, St. Petersburg, Russia; Dan Hagedorn, Seattle Museum of Flight; Alan Renga, San Diego Air & Space Museum; Carolyn Mars, Seattle Museum of History and Industry; the reference librarians in the Business, Sciences, and Technology Department at the Seattle Public Library; Von Hardesty and Carl Bobrow at the National Air and Space Museum.

Individuals who provided technical support and guidance to us need to be recognized as well. Gena Woodling, for her valuable assistance to us in understanding the nuances of photo management, editing and printing, Vladimir Titov for his superb artistic talent and patience in creating the book's cover art, and Andrey Karmazin for his beautiful color side-view drawings.

The authors are indebted to Jon Proctor, Cheryl Adamscheck, and Chuck Woodling for their critical reviews of our early manuscripts.

When it proved impossible for us to travel to libraries to study old and rare books, we relied on the Interlibrary Loan Department of the King County Public Library System to find those books and to obtain them for us on loan.

We reside eleven time zones apart from each other; therefore we could not have co-produced this book without access to the Internet. But there were many times when we needed to exchange hardcopy material and, thankfully many of our friends who travel internationally volunteered to transport the material for us. Special thanks in this regard are due to Richard Duncan, Anna Domnina, and Alexander Basyuk.

Finally, the authors wish to thank Schiffer Publishing for agreeing to publish this book. We have been researching the material for this book for over eight years and we are very glad to finally see it in print! We hope you enjoy the book!

Book design by Robert Biondi.

Printed in China.
ISBN: 978-0-7643-3762-8

We are always looking for people to write books on new and related subjects. If you have an idea for a book, please contact us at the address below.

Published by Schiffer Publishing Ltd.
4880 Lower Valley Road
Atglen, PA 19310
Phone: (610) 593-1777
FAX: (610) 593-2002
E-mail: Info@schifferbooks.com.
Visit our web site at: www.schifferbooks.com
Please write for a free catalog.
This book may be purchased from the publisher.
Please include $5.00 postage.
Try your bookstore first.

In Europe, Schiffer books are distributed by:
Bushwood Books
6 Marksbury Ave.
Kew Gardens, Surrey TW9 4JF
England
Phone: 44 (0)20 8392-8585
FAX: 44 (0)20 8392-9876
E-mail: info@bushwoodbooks.co.uk
www.bushwoodbooks.co.uk

CONTENTS

INTRODUCTION

On a good day it had a maximum speed of sixty miles per hour and a minimum speed of around forty miles per hour. Its bare-bones structure was composed of bamboo, ash, spruce, linen, and a few small pieces of metal and wire cables that held it all together. Its 500 cubic inch displacement V8 engine had a maximum output of seventy-five horsepower and was prone to overheating and sudden stoppages due to failed magnetos, spark plugs and drive train parts. No flying instruments were available to the pilot – no airspeed indicator, altimeter, turn-and-bank indicator or engine instruments. The pilot had to fly the airplane by the "seat-of-the-pants" method.

In spite of its problems, the spindly little Curtiss floatplane represented the cutting edge of aeronautical technology in 1911. The Navy was quick to seize the opportunity that the little airplane provided for the service to test the capabilities of an airplane in a naval environment. The Navy had that opportunity because a few forward-looking individuals had invested their time, money and intellects to develop a practical airplane, and they did it without government contracts.

Besides the early airplane designers' skill and daring, the role of serendipity cannot be overlooked as an enabling force in the development of the Navy's first airplane. The timely involvement of several influential people who promoted technology development in the early-1900s can only be attributed to good timing or good luck!

The book traces the development of the Navy's first airplane, the Curtiss Hydroaeroplane, from the early design and development efforts of Glenn Curtiss to the in-service Navy trials that were conducted by a small group of young and enthusiastic Navy and Marine officers. The airplane logbooks of the Navy's first two airplanes provide a very interesting and detailed commentary on the issues that those officers encountered in preparing the airplanes for service as a tool for training the cadre of aviators that became the core asset for future Navy air power.

The early operations by the some of the world's navies are documented in the book. Having barely entered service with the U.S. Navy, the Hydroaeroplane quickly became battle-tested during the 1914 Mexican-U.S. conflict at Veracruz, becoming the first U.S. military airplane inflicted with battle damage. Other navies that purchased the Curtiss Hydroaeroplane employed it primarily as a trainer, but one of those navies, The Imperial Russian Navy, equipped some of their airplanes with bomb racks at the beginning of World War I.

Glenn Curtiss simultaneously developed a successful commercial version of the Hydroaeroplane, and several individuals purchased the airplane for personal use or for making a profit by barnstorming across the country. Some of those individuals have very interesting histories. In fact, it is a very real possibility that The Boeing Company owes its existence to one of those characters and his privately owned Hydroaeroplane.

A significant portion of this book is dedicated to a detailed description of the design of the airplane and its Curtiss engine. To illustrate these designs, we have included newly created engineering drawings that are based on several years of painstaking research conducted on actual museum articles and scores of archival records. Chapter 6 also contains pilot reports and interesting period photos of the airplane.

Fortunately, one of the original Curtiss Hydroaeroplanes has survived and is on display in a museum in Cleveland, Ohio. Several reproductions of the Hydroaeroplane are currently on display in museums in the United States and one example is known to exist in Venice, Italy. We have visited all of these museums and have included photos of these airplanes.

Finally, we salute the U.S. Navy on its centennial year of Naval Aviation. The airplane described in this book set the stage for the creation of the world's most powerful naval air arm.

CHAPTER 1

Glenn Curtiss: the Innovative Yankee from New York

Glenn Hammond Curtiss (May 21, 1878 - July 23, 1930)
Harris & Ewing Collection, Prints & Photographs Division, Library of Congress, LC-DIG-hec-18631.

The Daredevil, the Dirigible, and the Deaf Woman

The Navy's first airplane was in some ways the product of seemingly unconnected personalities of vastly different interests and social status. That those people ever became connected appears to be a miracle of sorts. Three people who played a key role in the beginnings of the miracle are described here.

The Daredevil

Glenn Hammond Curtiss is known as the inventor of the first practical seaplane and the builder of the Navy's first airplane. His success as a world class aviation person could not have been predicted by his humble beginnings in the sleepy upstate New York town of Hammondsport. Located on the south end of Lake Keuka, the little town is miles away from any large city and in the early-1900s was known mainly for its production of wine.

The young Glenn Curtiss was a very bright student and excelled in mathematics, but his real love was racing; and racing just about anything, but mainly bicycles. He loved the exhilaration of speed and the joy of winning races. He was the consummate tinkerer and when it came to fixing things he was at his best. When it became obvious that his competitors were starting to beat Glenn, he decided to put a gasoline motor on his bicycle and get ahead of the pack for good.

Starting with an engine block that he purchased in 1901 from a mail order catalog, he put together an engine that ran – barely. After further tinkering and making modifications he was able to get the engine to run. His first test run of the engine on a bicycle was a complete success. The noise from the muffler-less engine must have woken up the Hammondsport townsfolk. Curtiss continued to refine the motor and the way in which it was attached to the bicycle. The third generation of motors was very well refined and performed superbly on the bicycle.

Because of his success with the motor-bicycle, other racers asked if they could buy one of the engines from Curtiss. The inquiries became so frequent that he went into the full-time business of building motorcycles. A production plant was built in Hammondsport on a hill above Glenn's grandmother's house. The motorcycle plant was later expanded to eventually become the Curtiss Aeroplane and Motor Company. The Glenn Curtiss Memorial School is now located on the property.

By 1903 Curtiss had become well known in the motorcycle-racing world, having won practically every event that he entered. In Yonkers, NY, he set a world's record of 64 mph on a motorcycle with a two-cylinder engine. In 1904 he set the speed record for a 10-mile course, averaging 67 mph. That record stood for seven

Glenn Curtiss and the V8 powered motorcycle that he rode to set a land speed record of 136.36 mph in 1907. *Courtesy of the Glenn H. Curtiss Museum, Hammondsport, NY.*

years. Curtiss continued to set speed records for motorcycles while continuously improving his engines.

His final motorcycle speed record was set in 1907 when he attached a 40 hp V8 engine of his own design to a specially built motorcycle and raced it at Ormond Beach, Florida. He set a world speed record for land vehicles of 136.36 mph. The record was not officially classified in the motorcycle category because it was felt that the engine was too large for the motorcycle category. The record stood for three years before being beaten by Bob Burman, driving a 200 hp Benz automobile.

The Dirigible

The word evokes images of the giant German Zeppelins that plied the skies in the early 20th century, but in the late nineteenth century the word was applied to a class of gas-filled balloons that could be maneuvered by a pilot. As an adjective, the word means "steerable," deriving its meaning from the Latin word *dirigere*. Thcsc aircraft were typically called dirigibles or dirigible balloons. Free balloons had existed for many years and had been used in combat in the Civil War and onboard Navy ships as a spotting aid for the fleet. Free ballooning had also been taken up by the public as a recreational sport and as a showman's entertainment device.

Because the dirigible balloons predated heavier than air machines, they held a special fascination for the public because of their ability to maneuver, almost independently of the wind. It was considered a great feat when a dirigible balloon could make a flight and return to the spot from which it had taken off. A lightweight gasoline engine was an essential feature of the dirigibles but the internal combustion engine was only beginning to come into its own as a reliable source of power.

One of the dirigible balloon pioneers was Thomas S. Baldwin, a former trapeze artist who, starting in 1885 began using a free balloon as a platform for his parachute jumps. He toured the country with his parachute act for many years, and later dubbed himself the "Father of the Modern Parachute."

Seeking to find a more daring act, Baldwin chose to develop a dirigible balloon. His dirigible's engine was a poor performer, causing him to cancel some of his appearances when the engine would not start. One day he noticed a Curtiss motorcycle and was impressed with the engine's reliability and light weight. He ordered an engine from the Curtiss factory and after becoming impatient with its delayed delivery, traveled to Hammondsport to meet with Curtiss. That meeting was

Thomas S. Baldwin, showman, balloonist and inventor who purchased Curtiss motorcycle engines to power his dirigible balloons. Baldwin introduced Curtiss to the world of powered flight. *Harris & Ewing Collection, Library of Congress Prints and Photographs Division, LC-H261-3339.*

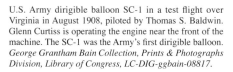

Thomas S. Baldwin's dirigible balloon *California Arrow* piloted by aeronaut Roy Knabenshue in its first successful flight at the St. Louis World's Fair, October, 1905. *Library of Congress Prints and Photographs Division, LC-USZ62-15815.*

U.S. Army dirigible balloon SC-1 in a test flight over Virginia in August 1908, piloted by Thomas S. Baldwin. Glenn Curtiss is operating the engine near the front of the machine. The SC-1 was the Army's first dirigible balloon. *George Grantham Bain Collection, Prints & Photographs Division, Library of Congress, LC-DIG-ggbain-08817.*

the beginning of a successful business relationship between Baldwin the dirigible driver and Curtiss the engine supplier.

Baldwin's first successful dirigible, the *California Arrow*, consisted of a 52-foot long sausage-shaped gas bag made of Japanese silk that had been treated inside and out to prevent gas leakage. Hanging under the gas bag was a long wooden truss that was triangular in cross-section and housed a small two-cylinder Curtiss engine amidships. The pilot moved fore and aft in this open truss, to make the dirigible rise or descend. The propeller was in front, connected to the engine by a long shaft. At very low speeds a large rudder in the rear provided directional stability and control, but at higher speeds the dirigible reportedly became unstable.

On August 3, 1904 in Oakland, California the *California Arrow* became the first airship to take off and land at the same spot. Given the success of his invention, Baldwin took the dirigible to the St. Louis World's Fair in the fall of 1904 where his pilot, Roy Knabenshue demonstrated the airship to a captivated audience of thousands.

Over the next few years Baldwin built several dirigibles at his business in San Francisco and demonstrated them across the country. The 1906 San Francisco earthquake and fire destroyed his business, including two of his dirigibles, the *California Arrow* and the *City of Portland*. Luckily, his second *California Arrow* dirigible had already been shipped to Hammondsport where Curtiss installed a larger air-cooled engine. Baldwin set up shop in Hammondsport where he completed the second *California Arrow*, which included innovative counter-rotating propellers. It was in this machine that Glenn Curtiss first took to the air, piloting the craft over Hammondsport on June 28, 1907. Curtiss easily handled the dirigible and was quoted as not being fearful of flying, but he was disappointed with the machine's slow speed. The daredevil had met the dirigible and he had mastered it.

The Army Signal Corps became interested in the airship idea and awarded Baldwin a $6,740 contract to supply a dirigible to demonstrate its abilities as a military vehicle. At Hammondsport Baldwin created his largest dirigible, one that was 96 feet long and powered with a new 4-cylinder water-cooled Curtiss engine. The contract specified a two-man crew for the dirigible, which was required to

demonstrate an endurance of two hours and a maximum speed of 20 mph. During August 1908 Baldwin, with Curtiss acting as his copilot and engine operator, successfully demonstrated the machine at Ft. Myer and on selected courses over the Virginia countryside. The Army purchased Baldwin's dirigible and named it SC-1 (Signal Corps Dirigible Number 1).

Baldwin went on to build two more dirigibles before deciding to build his own airplane. In 1909 he built a scaled-down version of the SC-1 and attempted to fly it from New York City to Albany. The attempt failed and he packed up the dirigible and headed back to the show circuit.

Curtiss had gained a lot of valuable information about the building and operation of lightweight and reliable aero engines, something that would be a key to his next life's adventure, the designing airplanes.

The Deaf Woman

Mabel Hubbard Bell seems an unlikely person to have become the facilitator for Glenn Curtiss's success as an airplane designer and manufacturer. Born into a wealthy Boston family, Mabel became totally deaf at age five after she contracted scarlet fever. Her future husband, Alexander Graham Bell, had moved from Scotland to Canada and finally, to Boston where he taught the deaf how to vocalize. Bell tutored Mabel, who was very intelligent and a skilled lip reader. They married in 1877, shortly after Bell received his patent for the telephone and after founding the Bell Telephone Company.

Mabel Hubbard Bell, wife of Alexander Graham Bell. Mrs. Bell financed the Aerial Experiment Association and encouraged its successful creation of innovative flying machines. *Harris & Ewing Collection, Prints & Photographs Division, Library of Congress, LC-DIG-hec-17777.*

Mabel's physical appearance was once described as "a slender, graceful woman, with the gentlest manners, her sweet sympathetic face framed in the most beautiful soft brown hair, a picture of elegance, skin smooth and white, graceful."

How Mabel Bell became the catalyst for Curtiss's airplane career will be explained after some background information on her husband's fascination with manned flight.

In 1896 Alexander Graham Bell witnessed the flight of one of Samuel Langley's early model flying machines and became convinced of the practicality of what he called "mechanical" flight. An ambitious inventor, Bell kept himself busy by experimenting with all sorts of devices to achieve "mechanical" flight. After a series of experiments on lifting surfaces and propellers, he began experiments with kites of various designs and in 1899 he perfected a triangular variation of the box kite.

In 1902 Bell created a kite with a tetrahedral cell composed of three triangles joined together to form a pyramidal structure. He continued his kite experiments with multiple tetrahedral cells joined together. By doing this Bell was able to prove that it was feasible to construct a large kite, of any size desired, without any increase in the weight to lifting surface area. Additional bracing is not required in larger kites and the strong tetrahedral cell is itself fully braced. In fact the more cells you add to the kite, the stronger it becomes. This allows one to build tetrahedral cells from the lightest materials but still have a strong and sturdy integrated structure.

Each kite had different surfaces of the tetrahedrons covered with silk to determine how the surfaces affected the kite's aerodynamics.

In 1904 Bell received a patent for his multi-cellular kite, titled "Aerial Vehicle or Other Structure." The patent award stimulated him to create a very large multi-cellular kite that would be able to support a man. The next year he demonstrated that his 1300-celled kite, the "Frost King," could support a man. The height achieved by the brave man was approximately 30 feet above the ground.

Alexander Graham Bell, inventor of the telephone, who became chairman of the Aerial Experiment Association in 1907. He provided overall leadership to the AEA and made his extensive laboratories available for the Association's use. *Harris & Ewing Collection, Prints & Photographs Division, Library of Congress, LC-DIG-hec-15688.*

Bell met Glenn Curtiss for the first time in New York in January 1906 at the Aero Club of America's first exhibit. Bell later ordered one of Curtiss's two-cylinder engines with the aim of using it to power one of his large tetrahedral kites. By the spring of that year Curtiss had delivered the engine to Bell's Nova Scotia summer home, where the engine was used for experiments. The engine proved difficult to operate and Bell asked Curtiss to come to Nova Scotia to improve the engine's performance, but Curtiss was too busy with his motorcycle business.

Bell ordered a larger 40 hp engine from Curtiss in early 1907 and persuaded him to personally deliver the engine to Nova Scotia. Curtiss arrived at Baddeck, Nova Scotia on July 13 and became a houseguest at Beinn Bhreagh, the Bell summer home.

Bell was ready to push ahead with his plans for a powered tetrahedral flying machine that could carry a man aloft and he had assembled a small team of young men to assist him in the design. In addition to Curtiss, F.W. "Casey" Baldwin, J.A. Douglas McCurdy and 1st Lieutenant Thomas E. Selfridge, of the U.S. Field Artillery were all resident at Beinn Bhreagh. Baldwin and McCurdy had recently received engineering degrees from Toronto University and both had worked with Bell the previous summer on tetrahedral structures. Selfridge was a young West Point graduate who had participated in commanding forces in San Francisco after the 1906 earthquake.

As Curtiss busied himself with the installation of the new engine with help from Baldwin and McCurdy, Mrs. Bell had developed an idea that would propel these men into new and exciting careers. It occurred to her "what a fine thing it would be to unite these unusual men with their different abilities into still closer relations." She suggested that they form themselves into an association with the aim of "getting into the air."

She added that she would be willing to fund the association with her own money! Dr. Bell agreed heartily with Mabel's proposal and the Aerial Experiment Association was born on October 1, 1907. Over the next few years Mabel allocated $35,000 of her own private wealth to the Association. Today her contribution would be worth the equivalent of over $800,000.

The Aerial Experiment Association and its Airplanes

Dr. Bell became chairman; Curtiss was elected chief executive and director of experiments and the headquarters of the Association was subsequently moved to Hammondsport. The parties agreed to work together for one year (later extended to 18 months).

The AEA began its work on the basis that each of the members would be responsible for the design of his own individual aircraft. Bell had no preconceived notions about what each aircraft would look like, but he asked that the first AEA aircraft be the tetrahedral kite machine that he was in the process of constructing. Bell's massive kite was composed of over 3,000 tetrahedral cells. In preparation for the first powered flight of the kite, dubbed *Cygnet I*, a towing test of the vehicle was performed on a lake in Nova Scotia. The *Cygnet I*, with Lt. Selfridge aboard rose to a height of 168 feet, but when it descended it was dragged through the water and

A glider was the Aerial Experiment Association's first flying machine. Shown here at Hammondsport in January 1908. *Photograph courtesy of the Canada Aviation Museum, Ottawa.*

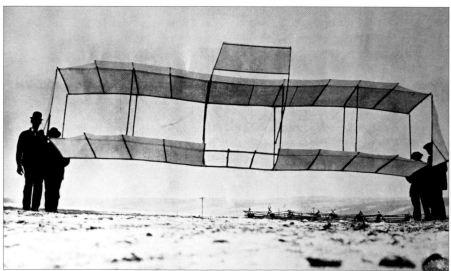

The *Red Wing* was the AEA's first powered airplane, shown here on the ice at Lake Keuka, March 1908. A Curtiss 40 hp air-cooled V8 powered the machine, that had a wingspan of 43 ft. 4 in. *Photograph courtesy of the Canada Aviation Museum, Ottawa.*

was destroyed. Further work on the tetrahedral concept was deferred and all work was transferred to Hammondsport.

The Association's first flying machine was a glider used to train the members in the basics of flight and to give them some experience in the design and construction of lightweight aircraft structures. The glider was a basic biplane design with an aft mounted vertical and horizontal tail similar to the designs published by Octave Chanute. Flight-testing began in January 1908 in the cold New York winter. The young aviators survived their gliding experience with only bumps and bruises and were ready to move on to the design of their first powered machine. The glider was destroyed in a bad landing while being tested as a kite and it was not rebuilt.

Red Wing

The AEA's first powered airplane (officially called *Aerodrome no.1*) was named *Red Wing,* so called because of the red silk covering used on its flying surfaces. Selfridge designed it at Bell's request, probably giving the young Lieutenant a reward for the dunking he received during the *Cygnet I* towing test. All of the members contributed to the design and construction, and the airplane was ready for its first flight on March 9, 1908, but did not fly until March 12. The airplane was designed with sled-type runners so it could be flown off the ice of Lake Keuka. Curtiss' 40 hp air-cooled V8 powered the machine, that had a wingspan of 43 ft. 4 in.

The *Red Wing's* first flight was piloted by Casey Baldwin, who flew the airplane to a height of 10 to 20 feet, at which point the right side of the tail buckled and the airplane rolled to the right, impacting the ice. Short as it was, the flight was the first public demonstration of powered flight in the U.S., the Wright Brothers having conducted their flights mostly in secret and unannounced.

The *Red Wing* was repaired and flown once more on March 17 with more disastrous results. Because the Red Wing did not have any lateral control devices, Baldwin was unable to counteract a roll caused by a gust of wind. The airplane simply rolled over onto its side and was demolished.

White Wing

The next AEA airplane (*Aerodrome no.2*) was designed by Casey Baldwin and was named *White Wing* because the wing surfaces were covered with white muslin material. Important new features of the *White Wing* were the wing tip control devices (ailerons) that were added at the suggestion of Dr. Bell. It was clear from the accident to the

The second AEA flying machine, *White Wing*, poised for takeoff at Hammondsport on May 18, 1908, piloted by Casey Baldwin. Moveable triangular surfaces have been added to the wing tips to provide lateral control. *Photograph courtesy of the Canada Aviation Museum, Ottawa.*

Red Wing that some means of lateral control was required. At Dr. Bell's suggestion Curtiss changed the lateral control system to include cables attached to the pilot's seat that moved the ailerons when the pilot leaned either to the right or left, toward the direction he wanted to turn. Dr. Bell felt this was a natural way to control the ailerons, and this feature continued to be used on Curtiss aircraft for many years.

The Wright brothers used wing warping for lateral control of their airplanes and they claimed that the AEA's use of ailerons infringed on their patent. The legal battle over the alleged patent infringement would last for many years and was not finally settled until 1917, when the government intervened and forced the cross-licensing of patents among the aircraft manufacturers.

Another new feature of the *White Wing* was the incorporation of a wheeled undercarriage, something that was needed because the ice had melted on Lake Keuka and further experiments had to be undertaken on land. It was a tricycle arrangement with a steerable front wheel. Curtiss later wrote that the forced move away from the wide-open spaces of the lake caused him to start thinking about an airplane designed with floats. The *White Wing*'s engine was a 40 hp air cooled Curtiss V8.

The first flight of the *White Wing* was made on May 18, 1908 piloted by Casey Baldwin. A short flight of 93 yards at a height of 20 feet was cut short when the flexible lower wing surface interfered with the propeller. Repairs were made overnight, and Selfridge made two short distance flights the following day of 100 ft. and 237 ft.

Dr. Bell was very happy with the *White Wing* flights and wrote: "The members of the Aerial Experiment Association are encouraged to believe that the engine has abundant power, and that the machine is under good control in the air, so that skill alone on the part of the aviator is all that is needed to accomplish much longer flights."

Curtiss's two flights in the *White Wing* on May 22 were his first experience in piloting an airplane. The airplane achieved and altitude of 10 ft and flew for a total of 339 yards. The AEA members were clearly feeling their way into powered flight, taking measured steps with their airplanes.

McCurdy flew the airplane on May 23 and after achieving a height of 20 ft, caught the right wingtip on the ground and the airplane crashed, slightly injuring McCurdy but destroying the airplane. Work began immediately on the next "Aerodrome," one that was designed by Glenn Curtiss.

June Bug

The AEA team continued to refine their airplanes, with *Aerodrome no.3* being designed by Glenn Curtiss and completed on June 19. The airplane was an evolution

of the *White Wing,* which was an evolution of the *Red Wing.* Dr. Bell named the airplane *June Bug* after the month in which it was created. Curtiss installed a V8 engine with a bit more horsepower, changed the arrangement of the ailerons, and increased the spacing of the main landing gear to provide more stability on the ground. He also adopted a modular assembly philosophy for the wings by making the outboard wing panels separate pieces that attached to a fixed wing center section.

Glenn Curtiss lifting off the ground at Hammondsport in the AEA's *June Bug*, the AEA's third airplane. On July 4, 1908 Curtiss used the airplane to capture the Scientific American trophy for the first airplane to fly one kilometer in a straight line. *Photograph courtesy of the Canada Aviation Museum, Ottawa.*

The first flight of the *June Bug* was attempted at Hammondsport on June 20, 1908 but Curtiss could not get the airplane to lift off because the wing's cloth covering was too porous. Applying a coat of "dope" that consisted of paraffin and gasoline eliminated the porosity. The paraffin was melted and poured into five parts of gasoline and allowed to cool before applying to the surfaces. In addition, the propeller was cut down 1.5 ft. on each tip, allowing the engine rpm to increase.

Curtiss made three successful flights on the evening of June 21 of 152, 139 and 422 yards, all of which lasted no more than 11 seconds. Another flight was attempted the next day but again the airplane would not lift off the ground because of porosity of the wing's covering material. The dope formula was changed to include turpentine and yellow ochre was added for photography purposes. The dope was then applied before it was allowed to cool. Curtiss resumed flying on June 25, but longitudinal control was difficult so Curtiss shut down the engine and landed after a flight of 725 yards that lasted 41 seconds. The front and rear control surfaces were increased in area, and a second flight of 1,140 yards was made that evening. The AEA team kept experimenting with the size of the control surfaces and Curtiss made two more short flights on June 27. The ailerons were exercised and slight turns were accomplished. By July 3 the *June Bug* had made 13 flights, giving Curtiss increasing confidence in his ability to fly the airplane.

Having confidence in their new machine's flying capabilities, the AEA team decided to attempt a flight to win the Scientific American trophy for the first airplane to fly one kilometer (about 1,100 yards) in a straight line. The attempt was scheduled for July 4 at Hammondsport and was attended by members of the Aero Club of America who were the official witnesses to the attempt. With Curtiss as the pilot, a flight of 2,000 yards was accomplished, far exceeding the requirements for the trophy. The flight was not exactly front-page news (the *New York Times* article was on page 5), but the AEA team was clearly ecstatic about its success and was ready to move on to their next airplane.

Bell recognized the importance of the event and immediately asked his law firm to examine the *June Bug* for features that could be patented. After much discussion with the law firm, a patent application was made for a "Flying-Machine" that included almost all of the features of the *June Bug* with emphasis on the ailerons and lateral control system. The U.S. patent, number 1,011,106, was awarded jointly to all the AEA members.

The AEA team continued flying the *June Bug* and on July 10 Curtiss flew the airplane in a complete circle. By the end of July they were ready to begin the construction of *Aerodrome no.4*, the *Silver Dart*. The airplane was to be the design of McCurdy with the help of only Curtiss because Baldwin left for Nova Scotia to work on Bell's tetrahedral machines and Lt. Selfridge was ordered to Washington DC to advise the newly formed Aeronautical Board of the Army. Meanwhile Curtiss was working on the SC-1 dirigible with Thomas Baldwin.

The AEA's work was drastically impacted on September 17 when Lt. Selfridge died in an airplane crash. He had been sent to Ft. Myer to observe the Wrights' airplane during its trials for the Army and he flew as a passenger on the airplane piloted by Orville Wright. During the flight a propeller broke and fouled the controls at which time Orville switched off the engine and turned the airplane back toward the field. The airplane stalled and crashed, killing Selfridge and seriously injuring Orville.

Loon

The *Aerodrome no.4* was named *Silver Dart* because of the silver-colored rubberized silk that was used to cover the wings. The *Silver Dart* was to be a larger and heavier machine than the *June Bug* and as such needed a more powerful engine. While the engine was being developed, McCurdy and Curtiss designed and built the airframe for the *Silver Dart*. While waiting for the completion of the new engine, there was a period in the fall of 1908 when there was nothing for their skilled workmen to work on. The idea of transforming the *June Bug* into a water-borne aircraft appealed to both Curtiss and McCurdy and work began that November.

Two lightweight floats, each 20 feet long and covered with rubberized cloth supported the *Loon*. The first water taxi tests began in late November but in every attempt, McCurdy could not get the *Loon* to lift off the water, even with the new, more powerful engine that was intended to be installed in the *Silver Dart*. Work was halted on the *Loon* and full attention was directed toward the *Silver Dart*. McCurdy and Curtiss agreed that the experiment had met with some success and told Bell that they hoped to work on the concept again after the *Silver Dart* flight testing.

The *Loon* was an experimental floatplane that utilized the basic *June Bug* airframe. Two lightweight floats, each twenty feet long and covered with rubberized cloth supported the *Loon*. Testing in November 1908 failed to get the Loon to take off from Lake Keuka. Development was abandoned to continue work on the *Silver Dart*. *Courtesy of The Museum of Flight, Seattle, WA.*

Front view of the *Loon* on the surface of Lake Keuka, November 1908. *Courtesy of the Glenn H. Curtiss Museum, Hammondsport, NY.*

Silver Dart

With three airplane designs under their belts, the AEA's *Aerodrome no.4* evolved as the most sophisticated of the quartet and with the exception of the *June Bug* it was their most important product. All of the construction features were significantly more refined than the preceding three aircraft and a new, more powerful water-cooled Curtiss V8 engine powered the airplane. The engine had been tested thoroughly on the ground and on the *Loon* and after a longer than expected gestation period the engine was ready to power the *Silver Dart* into the air. John McCurdy made the first flight on December 6 at Hammondsport and followed up with flights on December 9 and 14. The airplane handled well, in part due to its larger ailerons and more responsive elevator control.

The *Silver Dart* and its engine were shipped to Baddeck, Nova Scotia where Dr. Bell's second tetrahedral kite *Cygnet II* (*Aerodrome no.5*) was waiting for the installation of the *Silver Dart's* engine. After a series of failed experiments on the *Cygnet II*, the engine was transferred back to the *Silver Dart*, which made the first Canadian flight of a heavier-than-air machine on February 23, 1909. McCurdy was at the controls that day, taking off from the ice on Bras d'Or Lake and travelling about one-half mile at an altitude of 10 to 30 feet. A longer flight of more than 4 miles was made the following day by McCurdy who reported that the flying characteristics were about perfect and the engine worked beautifully.

The Canadian government began to show an interest in the use of aircraft for military operations after a presentation to the Canadian Club by Dr. Alexander Graham Bell in the spring of 1909. However, funding was not available, so the government offered the use of Camp Petawawa, Ontario, including its men and equipment for aeronautical trials. The *Silver Dart* and its crew arrived in Petawawa

The final product of the Aerial Experiment Association, the *Silver Dart*, shown here at Hammondsport, N.Y. in October 1908. Flying the *Silver Dart* off the ice of Bras d'Or Lake, John McCurdy made the first Canadian flight of a heavier-than-air machine on February 23, 1909. *George Grantham Bain Collection, Prints & Photographs Division, Library of Congress, LC-DIG-ggbain-02334*

in June 1909. By 31 July, the fragile aircraft was assembled and ready for flight. The first four demonstration flights occurred without any problems. On the fifth flight, while landing McCurdy caught a wheel on a small rise of the ground and crashed. The *Silver Dart* never flew again.

The AEA's work was reaching a conclusion at the beginning of 1909, with each member desiring to go on to new endeavors. Curtiss felt that flying at exhibitions could be profitable because of the large prizes that were being offered for winning events. Presumably Bell was not totally in agreement with the idea of making a profit from flying exhibitions. Part of the reason may have been his desire to stay away from any potential patent infringement suits that the Wrights were threatening. The AEA had made great strides in a short time period and could justifiably claim that they had advanced the science of aeronautics through their efforts. The Association terminated its work by mutual agreement on March 31, 1909.

The Herring-Curtiss Company

Curtiss conducted discussions with wealthy New York aviation enthusiasts in early 1909 that ended with an agreement for Curtiss to build an airplane for the Aeronautic Society of New York for $5,000. In the middle of these discussions Curtiss became involved with Augustus M. Herring, a man well known in the aviation field at the time who claimed to own patents for airplanes that were worth a considerable amount of money. He claimed the patents predated the ones of the Wrights. In a deal that was probably brokered by the Aero Club, Curtiss and Herring formed the Herring-Curtiss Company, headquartered at Hammondsport. Curtiss invested the entire worth of his company into the partnership and Herring invested his patents, which later turned out to be of little value. The company lasted about one year and went into bankruptcy in early 1910.

Golden Flier

In spite of the difficulties between Curtiss and Herring, they managed to fulfill the contract for the Aeronautic Society of New York by delivering an aeroplane to them in late May 1909. The machine was nicknamed the *Golden Flier* and was displayed at the Aero Club's exhibition, but Curtiss did not fly the airplane. The name was derived from the rubberized yellow silk that covered the wings and the orange shellac on the wood parts.

Glenn Curtiss in the Herring-Curtiss *Golden Flier*, taking off from the old Morris Park racetrack in the Bronx on June 26, 1909. The *Golden Flier* is considered to be the first Curtiss airplane (Curtiss No.1). *George Grantham Bain Collection, Prints & Photographs Division, Library of Congress, LC-DIG-ggbain-04015.*

The *Rheims Racer* at Hammondsport prior to its shipment to Europe. The extended spars that were used for wing span experiments are still attached in this photo. They were removed prior to the races in France and Italy. The shorter span wing resulted in a very fast airplane compared to the competition. *George Grantham Bain Collection, Prints & Photographs Division, Library of Congress, LC-DIG-ggbain-08231.*

Curtiss needed to use the *Golden Flier* to improve his flying skills, because the short flights he made in the AEA airplanes had not added much to his flying experience. The *Golden Flier* was outfitted with a 4-cylinder 25 hp water-cooled engine that allowed him to stay in the air for much longer intervals compared to the AEA machines with their air-cooled engines that overheated quickly. Impressed with their new aircraft and its designer, the Aero Club chose Curtiss as the sole American entrant in the first international aviation meet that was to be held in Rheims, France in August 1909.

Rheims Racer

Curtiss knew that the *Golden Flier* that he had just delivered to the Aeronautic Society of New York was not capable of winning the Gordon Bennett Aviation race at the Rhiems meet in August. He therefore began building a machine that had characteristics similar to the *Golden Flier* but with a new, more powerful 50 hp V8 engine. Curtiss also reduced the wingspan to lower the aerodynamic drag and fine-tuned the control system. He was able to complete the new aircraft in four weeks, just enough time to do a one-day flight test before boarding a ship for France with his airplane, named the *Rheims Racer*.

The *Rheims Racer* performed beautifully in all of the events that Curtiss entered at Rheims. Curtiss competed in the Bennett Cup race on August 28 in which the *Racer* proved to be faster than the European airplanes, with Curtiss flying it around the 20-kilometer course at an average speed of 47 mph. That winning speed was enough for Curtiss to claim the Gordon Bennett Aviation Cup, its $5,000 prize money and instant notoriety as the fastest man in the air. Later Curtiss won a three-lap race and placed second in a one-lap race, losing a close race to Louis Bleriot. In all, his winnings at Rheims totaled $7,600.

From Rheims Curtiss travelled to Brescia, Italy with the *Rheims Racer* to participate in an air meet where he won all of the big events, taking home prize money totaling $9,000. Participating in the European air meets encouraged Curtiss to continue the lucrative business in the U.S., where the first big aviation meet was being planned for the Los Angeles area.

The Curtiss Aeroplane Company

When the Herring-Curtiss Company was dissolved in early 1910, Curtiss formed the Curtiss Aeroplane Company and separately, the Curtiss Exhibition Company. The two companies were formed for the purpose of profiting from the sales of airplanes and also the exhibition of airplanes to the public, which was growing ever more

Louis Paulhan taking off in his Farman biplane at the Los Angeles international air meet at Dominguez Field in January 1910. Paulhan took home the most prize money of all of the contestants in the air meet, primarily for endurance flights in his Farman and Bleriot airplanes. *George Grantham Bain Collection, Prints & Photographs Division, Library of Congress, LC-DIG-ggbain-04478.*

interested in seeing airplanes fly and compete in speed, distance and altitude events. In addition he established his own flight training schools in San Diego, Miami, and Hammondsport.

The "First in America Aviation Meet" was held from January 10th through the 20th at Dominguez, a city near Los Angeles. Curtiss, along with several U.S. and European aviators competed for prize money totaling $75,000 in a diverse number of events that were created to arouse interest of the public. The number of people who attended the events averaged about 20,000 per day, peaking at over 50,000 on the weekend days. Curtiss competed with the *Rheims Racer* and two 4-cylinder airplanes that were destined to be delivered to customers. As part of Curtiss's newly formed Exhibition Company, Charles Willard and Charles Hamilton also participated in the meet, Willard piloting the *Golden Flier* and Hamilton in another Curtiss biplane.

Louis Paulhan, a famous French aviator won the most amount of money during the meet, totaling $19,000, mostly for his endurance flights in his Farman and Bleriot airplanes. The Curtiss airplanes took their share of prizes as well, Curtiss alone earning over $6,000 in the speed trials and short takeoff events. The Los Angeles air meet was a huge success for the fledgling aviation industry and many more aviation meets were held in 1910, earning large sums of money for the aviators and for the airplane manufacturers. The newly formed Curtiss Aeroplane Company was swamped with orders for its airplanes

Canoe Machine

Curtiss continued to be interested in water-borne aircraft and in May 1910 he used one of the new biplanes to test flotation devices on Lake Keuka. His aim was to see if a single, centerline float could be made to work. Curtiss felt that twin floats similar to those on the Loon had too many disadvantages from an operational standpoint, so he began experimenting by attaching a canoe to one of his airplanes in place of its wheeled undercarriage. The main purpose of the experiment was to determine the balance point of the canoe/airplane combination. Curtiss never intended to fly the *Canoe Machine*, instead using it for water-borne taxi tests. The test became the basis for his decision to design a larger centerline float for the airplane that he took to San Diego late in 1910 for his initial hydroaeroplane tests.

Later, in 1916 he defended a patent infringement suit by using the same canoe, attached to a hydroaeroplane airframe to demonstrate that the canoe/airplane combination could be flown. The new airplane had three times as much horsepower as the original *Canoe Machine* engine, allowing Curtiss to fly the airplane off the surface of Lake Keuka for a short distance.

Albany Flier

Now one of the best known aviators in the world, Curtiss set out to capitalize on his fame by entering the most challenging contest in which he had ever competed. Offers were pouring into Hammondsport for Curtiss to conduct flying exhibitions across the country, but the first order of business was to compete for the *New York World's* $10,000 prize (over $200,000 today) for the first aircraft to fly between Albany and New York. The rules, as written by the newspaper specified that the prize would be awarded to the first person to duplicate, in the air, the trip of Robert Fulton's steamboat trip from New York to Albany in 1807. The contest was open to any "mechanically propelled airship," either lighter than air or heavier than air. The flight had to be completed within 24 consecutive hours and two intermediate landings were permitted for refueling. The flight could be made in either direction. To qualify for the prize the trip had to be completed on or before October 10, 1910.

Curtiss knew that he would need a reliable airplane and engine to navigate the 152 miles between Albany and New York. While the factory was building the new airplane, named *Albany Flier*, Curtiss scouted out the entire route, looking for places to land safely and refuel during the flight. He selected an open field near

The *D-II Canoe Machine* was Curtiss's second foray into the field of water-borne aircraft. The 4-cylinder engine was not powerful enough to allow the craft to lift off the waters of Lake Keuka, however Curtiss never intended to fly the *Canoe Machine*, instead using it for taxi tests on the lake in May 1910. *Courtesy of the Glenn H. Curtiss Museum, Hammondsport, NY.*

The *Albany Flier* was the airplane that solidified the early fame of Glenn Curtiss. He flew the airplane from Albany to New York City on May 29, 1910, winning the *New York World's* $10,000 prize for the first aircraft to fly between Albany and New York. Note the two auxiliary floats and the centerline bag filled with cork, extra precautions added in the event of an unplanned landing in the Hudson River. *Courtesy of the Museum of Flight, Seattle, WA.*

Poughkeepsie as the intermediate refueling point and scouted out landing spots on Manhattan Island in case he was not able to make it all the way to Governors Island, his preferred destination within the city limits of New York City.

The *Albany Flier* was designed for distance flying, as compared to the *Rheims Racer,* which was designed for speed, and as a consequence the *Albany Flier's* wingspan was increased substantially compared to the *Racer.* Curtiss preferred the name *Hudson Flier,* but popular opinion caused the *Albany Flier* name to stick. Curtiss was aware that there were very few suitable landing fields along the Hudson and that he might have to land on the river in an emergency. In anticipation of an unplanned water landing, he added two large metal canister-shaped floats to the underside of the lower wings. To be extra safe, he attached a large canvas bag filled with cork to the undercarriage frame. The airplane with its flotation devices attached was tow-tested in Lake Keuka, proving its somewhat marginal flotation capability, but it floated just high enough in the water to enable Curtiss to escape from the airplane if he had to land in the Hudson River.

The airplane was shipped to Van Rensselaer Island in the Hudson River at Albany where Curtiss planned to begin his flight to New York City. At 7:30 on the morning of May 29, 1910 Curtiss lifted off the island, immediately headed down the Hudson while climbing to 1,000 ft. above the river. One hour and 22 minutes later and 75 miles from Albany, he landed at Camelot, near Poughkeepsie to refuel the gas tank, and to inspect the airframe and engine. He took off about an hour later and was cruising in calm air until he was abeam West Point when a downdraft forced the airplane to descend to within 50 ft. of the river. The winds abated quickly as he flew south past the Palisades and he was excited when he first glimpsed the tall buildings on Manhattan Island. However, his elation quickly turned to fear when he turned around and discovered that the oil gauge on the crankcase indicated that the engine was low on oil. He decided to land on the north end of Manhattan Island at a little meadow at Inwood that he had found on his earlier scouting trip.

Curtiss went to a nearby telephone and called the *New York World* newspaper to report that he had arrived in New York City and planned to fly from Inwood to Governors Island. Someone fetched oil for him, a bystander swung the prop for him, and he took off for the short flight to Governors Island. Along the way thousands of people had become aware of Curtiss's flight and they were crowding the West Side of the island for a glimpse of the airplane. Boats on the Hudson sounded their sirens until the intrepid aviator reached the Statue of Liberty, which he circled before landing on Governors Island. Curtiss had flown the 152 miles between Albany and New York City at an average speed of 52 mph.

Almost every newspaper in the country carried a page-one account of the flight, which was by far the longest flight to that date. The $10,000 prize money that Curtiss collected from the *New York World* was a welcome shot in the arm for his new companies and the publicity that he received for the completing the flight resulted in many more orders for his airplanes.

The daredevil had once again captured the public's attention, and he was now more than ready to accept the challenges that would surely come his way in the following years.

CHAPTER 2

The U.S. Navy Places its Bet on Glenn Curtiss

One of the more important lessons learned from the work of the Aerial Experiment Association was the powerful effect that teamwork can play in the development of new ideas and inventions. On their own, the members of the AEA could not have achieved their goals without the help of the other members. Each member brought his own unique set of personal attributes to the Association. Each possessed strong leadership qualities but each of them was also willing to work as a team member in the pursuit of the Association's goals.

The men who created naval aviation practiced leadership styles of their own, sometimes leading by example and sometimes leading by the sheer force of their will. Each man seems to have innately understood his own unique role in the creation process, and worked cooperatively with others to provide a strong foundation on which naval aviation grew to become a powerful adjunct to the fleet.

The following is a chronology of the men and events that shaped the development of naval aviation in the incredibly short time period in 1910 and early 1911.

Captain Chambers in Charge

Captain Washington Irving Chambers was fifty-three years old when he assumed command of the battleship USS *Louisiana* in 1909. Chambers had an interesting and varied career prior to this assignment and was considered one of the corps of reformers in the officer ranks who fought for many years to transform the Navy into a modern fighting force. A native of Kingston, New York, he was the son of a boot maker and was named after the famous New York author, Washington Irving.

Chambers graduated from the naval academy in 1876, ranked twenty-eight out of the class of forty-two, having spent five years at the academy and repeating his first year. He developed many influential relationships at the academy and later in his career that would help him climb the Navy's ladder of promotion. He possessed an analytical mind and had submitted designs for advanced fleets of battleships and cruisers, based on the latest technologies and naval warfare tactics. He also spent a considerable amount of time working to improve the Navy's torpedoes and torpedo boats. In 1909 Chambers was well on his way toward promotion to admiral; having assumed command of a battleship, which was considered a prerequisite for promotion.

That same year, the supremely bureaucratic and highly political Navy Department was in the throes of a major reorganization, led by Secretary of the Navy George von L. Meyer. That year he created an umbrella organization consisting of four top aides who reported to him directly. The four had responsibility for Operations, Personnel, Inspections and Material.

Washington Irving Chambers in his commander's uniform prior to his promotion to captain in December 1908. Chambers is viewed by many as the father of U.S. Naval aviation, having led the Navy's effort to acquire its first aircraft. *Harris & Ewing Collection, Prints & Photographs Division, Library of Congress, LC-DIG-hec-15899.*

Admiral William H. Swift was put in charge of Material, an organization that included the bureaus of Construction and Repair, Engineering, Ordnance, and Equipment. Admiral Swift was quick to seize the opportunity to make the voice of the line officers heard in the design and operation of the fleet's ships. He felt he needed an aide who had an analytical mind and could infuse some rigor and judgment into the design of the Navy's fleet, while at the same time dealing with the squabbling bureaus that had just been placed in his command.

Admiral Swift asked Chambers to fill the role of aide for the design and construction of Navy ships. He requested that Chambers leave his newly acquired command of the *Louisiana* and report to Washington to join the admiral's staff. Chambers was reluctant to leave his new command, but Swift insisted that Chambers was needed immediately to oversee the development of the new organization. Ultimately Chambers accepted the new position, assuming that he would soon return to sea duty, and an expected eventual promotion to admiral.

Chambers set to work encouraging more cooperation among the bureaus and within a short time streamlined the administration of the groups that reported to the Navy Secretary's Aide for Material.

As early as 1908 the Navy expressed some interest in the airplane, an invention that had captured the imagination of the general public and also the U.S. Army. The Wright brothers were anxious to promote the newly refined version of the airplane that they first flew in late 1903. In September 1908, the brothers demonstrated their invention to the army at Ft. Myer, Virginia. The Navy sent a lieutenant and a naval constructor to Ft. Myer to witness the flight demonstration. The pair produced an enthusiastic report on what they witnessed and recommended the purchase of airplanes as soon as possible.

The demonstration resulted in an airplane purchase by the Army but not the Navy. Secretary Meyer had a low opinion of the small and fragile Wright aircraft. By 1910, however, other noted designers like Glenn Curtiss had created more advanced aircraft designs and participated in more interesting flight demonstrations and exhibitions.

Glenn Curtiss's Aerial Demonstrations

Glenn Curtiss, in particular, captured newspaper headlines in May 1910 by flying down the Hudson River from Albany to New York City and winning a $10,000 prize offered by the *New York World*. The nation's newspapers printed many articles about the flight, making comparisons between the Hudson River course and the flight made by Louis Bleriot across the English Channel in 1909. Some newspapers even extrapolated the capability of the airplane as being able to fly across the Atlantic.

USS *Michigan* (Battleship #27) circa 1916-1917. She and her sister ship, USS *South Carolina* were the first U.S. Navy ships built in the "dreadnought" era. The two tall basket masts supported platforms for spotters who tracked the long range 12-inch gun shells. *U.S. Naval History and Heritage Command Photograph. Photo no. NH 106438*

The Hudson flight also opened the eyes of the Navy to the capabilities of the airplane to conduct enemy fleet scouting missions and to act as the target spotters for the big guns on the Navy's battleships. As the battleships' guns grew in size with time, the range of the guns' projectiles also increased, making it more difficult for ship-based crews to act as reliable spotters. The thought of the airplane being more than a scout or observer did not seem to interest the Navy. As an offensive weapon, the light and fragile aircraft of the day could hardly carry bombs large enough to inflict serious damage on a ship of the line, the Navy believed.

Nevertheless, primitive bombing demonstrations were conducted by Glenn Curtiss to convince the Navy of the versatility of his airplane designs. In June, 1910 the *Washington Post* reported that Curtiss had conducted simulated bombings of a battleship sized target near his home in Hammondsport, NY:

> Hammondsport, NY, June 30 – To demonstrate the effectiveness of the aeroplane in naval warfare Glenn Curtiss, the aviator, made several flights in a biplane over Lake Keuka today in the presence of Admiral Kimball, of the Navy Department, at Washington, and dropped 20 bombs at marks. He is credited with having hit the mark eighteen times in the twenty trials. Admiral Kimball is said to have expressed himself as greatly impressed with the possibilities of the aeroplane in warfare.

Curtiss's "battleship" target was very large and stationary so the demonstration was viewed by many as meaningless. The "bombs" that he dropped on the target were merely short lengths of metal pipe.

In July, Curtiss responded to criticisms about the large and stationary target that he "bombed" the previous month in Hammondsport. The following is a newspaper article describing his actions:

> Atlantic City, July 13 – Crossing the sailing line of the yacht John E. Mehre, 2d, used as a target in place of a battleship, Glenn Curtiss, using oranges as "bombs," gave an exhibition of his ability to drop high explosives on the deck of the craft. Fearing harm to the officials and ladies on the yacht, Curtiss placed his missiles so accurately alongside that spray was thrown over the gowns of the women. Then, whirling away, Curtiss took his plane far out to sea and beyond the range of anything but a twelve-inch gun, while the yacht passengers and watchers shuddered at the thought of the possibilities had the bombs been spheres of real explosives and the trim and glistening craft the object of real attack. "The trial shows absolutely that the day of the battleship for attack on foreign cities is nearing its end," declared Colonel William Allen Jones, U.S.A., retired, formerly of the engineer corps. "Curtiss could have dropped a bomb on the deck of even that small craft with just us much ease and certainty as he showed when he spun them close enough to the vessel to show his ability without endangering the people on board. As for hitting that swooping aeroplane from the deck of a battleship, it would be practically impossible except with rifle balls, and both driver and engine could be protected with the lightest sort of armor or bullet proof cloth," concluded the army official. Following his sham attack on the mock battleship, Curtiss dropped more orange "bombs" at a circular mark on the beach to show the ease with which he could hurl explosives into the camp of soldiers.

Later in July Curtiss established an over-water endurance record for airplanes by flying north and south off the beach at Atlantic City for more than one hour. He managed to fly about fifty miles in setting the record.

Chambers Prevails

All of the publicity had not escaped the attention of the secretary of the Navy, who instructed his aides to deal with the growing amount of correspondence that was arriving at the Navy. After all, the army ordered airplanes in 1909 but the Navy had shown virtually no interest in aviation despite the successful demonstrations of Curtiss and others. In September 1910, Captain Washington I. Chambers was given the added responsibility of overseeing "aviation correspondence."

Chambers' position was not well defined; he had no staff to support him and no official title and no authority. This probably suited the secretary, who still viewed airplanes as irrelevant to the Navy's needs. In spite of this, Chambers tackled his assignment with vigor, educating himself on the latest developments in aviation, both in the United States and abroad. He became aware of the large financial support that European governments were giving to the development of aviation and lobbied to establish a budget for the development of U.S. naval aviation. The Navy's General Board, headed by Admiral George Dewey, generally favored the funding of naval aviation, but the board had little influence on the secretary of the Navy and his four aides.

By late 1910, however, Admiral Dewey managed to convince the General Board to recommend that the design of a new scout cruiser include provisions for deploying an aircraft from the ship. Management of the airplane for this new cruiser program was split between the Bureau of Construction and Repair and the Bureau of Steam Engineering. The airframe became the responsibility of the Bureau of Construction and Repair but the Bureau of Steam Engineering was responsible for the aircraft engine. When the Navy finally ordered an airplane in 1911 from Curtiss, two contracts were let, one for the airframe and one for the engine.

The scheme of dividing the Navy's aviation responsibilities between the two bureaus greatly reduced Chambers' authority and responsibilities, although he nominally retained control over the overall strategy, policy making and personnel selection for naval aviation. Chambers had a difficult time dealing with the bureaus, and they frequently ignored him, dealing directly with the secretary of the Navy. However, each bureau was instructed to appoint an officer to coordinate with Chambers. The two men selected were Lieutenant Nathaniel Wright and Naval Constructor William McEntee. Chambers invited the two officers to accompany him to an aviation meet in New York. The purpose of the trip was to meet the world's top aircraft designers and aviators and inspect their airplanes.

The aviation meet was the last major U.S. air meet of 1910 and it took place October 22-31 at the large Belmont Park racetrack on Long Island, New York. The Belmont International Aviation Tournament offered approximately $75,000 in prize money and attracted one of the period's most talented fields of pilots. Events ranged from competitions for the best altitude, speed, and distance to contests for the most precise landing and the best mechanic.

More than two dozen of the world's top aviators attended the New York meet. They came from England, France and the United States. Key aviators from France included Count Jacques de Lesseps and Roland Garros. Claude Grahame-White came from England. The top American pilots included Glenn Curtiss, John Moisant, Arch Hoxsey, Ralph Johnstone and Charles Hamilton.

One famous Frenchman who did not attend was Henri Fabre, who made man's first successful takeoff from, and landing on, water on March 28, 1910. Although Fabre's hydroaeroplane was not exhibited at Belmont, it is likely that Chambers discussed the design with Curtiss and other aviators.

The Belmont air meet provided the perfect opportunity for Chambers, McEntee and Wright to inspect the latest technology in airframes and engines, and to discuss aviation issues with the designers of the aircraft and their pilots. They had discussions with Glenn Curtiss and Eugene Ely, his chief pilot at the time.

The World's First Seaplane

The first man in history to design and build an aircraft capable of taking off and landing on water was a little known Frenchman named Henri Fabre. Similar to many of the early French aviators, he was not an aviator by profession. His true profession was marine engineer, which may account for his success in designing the three-float configuration that his spindly invention relied on for flotation.

Fabre's invention could hardly be called an aircraft. It looked more like an unfinished conglomeration of spars to which a wing and various other appendages were attached. The fifty-horsepower Gnome rotary engine was mounted at the back, immediately aft of the wing and the rectangular fixed vertical tail. Below all this, on either side of the tail, were two streamlined hollow wooden floats. Fabre sat about midway on the top crosspiece of his flying framework of spars. Two elevators provided some degree of control; and beneath the forward elevators was a third float for balance. Additional control was maintained by pushing foot pedals that caused the tips of the wings to bend and twist, similar to the Wright's wing warping design.

The aircraft was stable in flight, a remarkable achievement considering Fabre's lack of aerodynamic expertise. The Gnome engine, which spun around at about one thousand rpm, did not have a throttle, and consequently, ran at two speeds: Off or On. Fabre's limited success with this pioneer seaplane is all the more remarkable, considering that several more experienced designers had failed in their attempts at water flying.

After a few such flights, and a bad dunking, Fabre gave up aviation while he was still alive. His contribution was not so much the design details as it was his proof that a seaplane could be built and flown.

Henri Fabre's *Canard* in flight at Monaco in April 1911, piloted by Jean Becu. Photo © *Musée de l'Air et de l'Espace/Paris-Le Bourget*

Henri Fabre's hydroaeroplane *Canard* in the water at Monaco in April 1911. Photo © *Musée de l'Air et de l'Espace/Paris-Le Bourget*

In early November 1910 the three Navy officers attended another air meet held at Halethorpe, Maryland, where they witnessed simulated bombings and again had discussions with Glenn Curtiss and Eugene Ely. Chambers doubted the ability of the airplane to inflict serious damage by dropping bombs on land or sea targets and therefore continued to promote their use solely for scouting and artillery spotting. To make his vision a reality Chambers knew he would have to demonstrate the ability of airplanes to be easily launched and recovered by Navy ships. During the air meet at Halethorpe, Eugene Ely spoke with Chambers about the feasibility of a takeoff from a ship and Ely readily volunteered to fly a Curtiss biplane from the platform on the USS *Birmingham*. Chambers originally solicited support for the attempt from the Wright brothers but they very emphatically turned him down. Wilbur Wright considered the attempt as too dangerous. Orville's 1909 crash at Ft. Myer that killed Army Lt. Thomas Selfridge undoubtedly influenced Wilbur's decision.

Curtiss was eager to help Chambers and offered to provide an airplane and pilot to demonstrate a takeoff from a Navy ship. The Navy would have to provide the ship and also finance the ship's modifications that would include a takeoff platform for the Curtiss airplane. Chambers set out to convince his superiors that such a demonstration was feasible and would provide valuable publicity for the Navy. Admiral Wainwright, the aide for operations, and the primary officer that Chambers needed to convince turned down Chambers' request for a ship. Ely personally appealed to Navy Secretary Meyer, but Meyer's low opinion of airplanes had not improved and he rejected their plea.

The Hamburg-America Line's *Pennsylvania* docked at New York City in November 1910, showing preparations for the launch of a Curtiss biplane from a temporary deck. A launch accident prevented the attempt from becoming the first shipboard launch of an airplane. *George Grantham Bain Collection, Prints & Photographs Division, Library of Congress, LC-DIG-ggbain-08732.*

Meanwhile, Curtiss had convinced the Hamburg-America steamship line that the publicity derived from an attempted takeoff from a ship was worth the cost and effort of taking one of its cruise ships out of service for a short time. Company managers agreed to provide their liner *Pennsylvania* to be modified for such an attempt. A plan was formulated in which the *Pennsylvania* would steam about fifty miles from New York harbor and launch the airplane, which would fly to Manhattan and land with a sack of mail to be delivered on arrival.

The attempted launch from the *Pennsylvania* was covered extensively by New York newspaper reporters, who published every small detail of the preparations. The attempt, originally planned for the beginning of November, was delayed several times. Finally, on November 12 the *Pennsylvania* was ready to depart the pier along with a Curtiss biplane that had been assembled on the makeshift takeoff deck. Glenn Curtiss personally inspected the airplane, only to discover that the gasoline tank had been accidentally filled with water. The tank was removed from the airplane and every drop of water was drained to Curtiss's satisfaction. Curtiss then suggested that the airplane's engine be started just to make sure that the water had been purged form the fuel system. Unfortunately, a small metal funnel that was carelessly left on the lower wing was sucked into the propeller and then thrown into the bamboo outriggers that held the tail section in place. The propeller and bamboo outrigger were badly damaged, and unfortunately no spares were available. The whole operation was cancelled, primarily because winter weather was approaching and the steamship line needed to place the *Pennsylvania* back into trans-Atlantic service.

Captain Chambers' Gamble

During the delays in the Hamburg-America line's launch attempt, and during a week when Secretary Meyer was out of the office, Chambers was able to use the steamship line's German nationality to persuade Meyer's stand-in to authorize the use of a Navy ship to demonstrate an airplane launch. The only problem was that the Navy had not budgeted the funds for the modifications that would be needed for the attempt.

Fortunately, John Barry Ryan, a millionaire publisher and politician, became involved in the appeal for the test. Two months earlier Ryan had organized financiers, investors and scientists interested in aeronautics, along with a few pilots, into a "United States Aeronautical Reserve." Curtiss was among those who had joined the Reserve. Ryan furnished this new paramilitary aviation group with a large Fifth Avenue clubhouse in New York City, provided several cash prizes for aeronautical achievements by its members, and named himself commodore of the organization. One of the prizes offered was $1,000 to the first Reserve member to complete a ship-to-shore flight of one mile or more. Ryan happened to be in Washington, lobbying to pledge the club's pilots and their planes to the Army and Navy in the case of war, when he heard of the Chambers-Ely plan and reopened the subject with Secretary Meyer.

John Barry Ryan, the wealthy aviation enthusiast who financed the modifications to the USS *Birmingham*, facilitating Eugene Ely's record-setting takeoff from the ship. Ryan also founded the U.S. Aeronautical Reserve, an organization that lobbied U.S. military planners in Washington DC. *George Grantham Bain Collection, Prints & Photographs Division, Library of Congress, LC-DIG-ggbain-05499*

When Ryan urged adoption of Chambers' proposal, Secretary Meyer responded that the Navy had no funds for aviation experiments. Ryan offered to withdraw the $1,000 prize that the non-member Ely could not win anyway, and use it to pay the Navy for the costs of the test. Meyer, an accomplished politician, knew that Ryan could help swing votes in the upcoming presidential election. So, after consulting with President Taft, he agreed that the Navy would furnish a ship, but no funds.

The cruiser USS *Birmingham* was immediately assigned to Captain Chambers and a rudimentary takeoff platform was hastily constructed over the ship's forecastle while it was docked at Norfolk, Virginia.

Ely's attempted takeoff from the *Birmingham* occurred on November 14, 1910, as described by Chambers in the following article that he wrote for a 1911 issue of *Proceedings*:

His aeroplane followed accurately the middle line mark on the platform, and its tail cleared the forward end by about 20 feet, before he gave it a graceful, bird-like swoop or volplane [glide] (to increase the speed) and then he gradually arose to a height variously estimated at 150 to 500 feet. In thus swooping down, the lower part of his machine, the skid framing and the pontoons, struck the water and was sufficiently submerged to demonstrate that if his speed had not already been accelerated to more than sufficient for flight, the retardation caused by the plunge would have prevented further flight. He explained later that his touching the water was entirely due to a miscalculation in moving the rod of the front control or elevator. His rod had been lengthened, since his previous use of it, to suit another aviator, and when he pulled it towards him to raise the elevator he did not give quite enough angle to the planes to prevent too deep a dive. On striking the water, the propeller tips struck also and both driving edges were splintered. This did not apparently affect the control or the speed of the aeroplane, and it demonstrated that such a propeller may be considerably damaged without affecting a flight seriously.

A quantity of salt water was splashed up over his goggles, and this, combined with the continued rain, rendered very obscure his view of the necessary landmarks that were further obscured by the thick weather. He accordingly became confused in his bearings, and after about four minutes in flight, seeing the broad beach on the north side of Willoughby Spit spread out invitingly under him, he decided to land there. This he did, in the soft sand, without any damage to the aeroplane, after a flight of 2 1/2 miles. I was pleased to learn that he had not continued on towards Norfolk, as I had begun to have grave doubts

Eugene Ely's 1910 takeoff from the USS *Birmingham* (Scout Cruiser #2) from a temporary platform erected over her forecastle. Ely made a short two mile flight, landing on a nearby beach rather than proceeding on to Norfolk, as planned. *Courtesy of the Naval Historical Foundation – Photo no. NH76511.*

about his ability to get his bearings in thick weather, over a landscape with which he was unfamiliar. After he had demonstrated his ability to leave the ship so readily, without assistance from the ship's speed, or from any special starting device, such as that formerly used by the Wright brothers, my satisfaction with the results of the experiment was increased, for two reasons:

> (1.) The point of greatest concern in my mind about carrying out the original program was the uncertainty of stopping the ship or changing the course in time to prevent running over the aviator in case he should land in the water.
> (2.) His demonstration, that an aeroplane of comparatively old design and moderate power can leave a ship in flight while the ship is not under way, points clearly to the conclusion that the proper place for the platform is aft. An after platform can be made longer, will not require a loosening of the stays of any mast, and its essential supports can be so rigged as a part of the permanent structure of a scout cruiser as to cause no inconvenience in arranging the other military essentials of the ship's design.

This information amply repays for the small expense of rigging the experimental platform. Furthermore, if it be desired to have an aeroplane land on board of the ship the after position of the platform is the best for that purpose. It would be comparatively easy, in smooth water, for a scout to steam head to wind at the proper speed to allow of the gradual approach and descent of an aeroplane to a platform located aft. Safety nets at each side of a middle runway could easily be rigged. If the condition of the wind and sea should render such a landing inadvisable, the aviator could land in the water under the lee of the ship and be picked up by a boat's crew.

Chambers was ecstatic over the results of the flight and stated: "Every cruiser should be equipped with planes. This experiment brings us up even with the other world powers in aviation progress. I do not believe that the aeroplanes will ever take the place of scouting cruisers, but I do believe that scouting cruisers will be made twice as valuable to the Navy, at small cost."

Secretary Meyer immediately sent a congratulatory letter to Ely. But in a separate letter to Curtiss, Meyer insisted that he could not consider the airplane as a useful machine to the Navy until Curtiss demonstrated the feasibility of landing an airplane alongside a battleship and retrieving it without the use of a supplementary deck on the ship.

Lt. Ellyson's Orders

It was now clear to Curtiss that a seaplane was what the Navy was really looking for and he immediately set out to design one. In a letter dated November 29, 1910, Curtiss invited the Army and Navy to send officers to the Curtiss training facility in San Diego for instruction in the care and operation of the Curtiss type of aeroplane. Curtiss's letter to Secretary Meyer included the following:

> To be of some assistance in developing the adaptability of the aeroplane to Military purposes, I am leaving for the Pacific Coast, where I have established a winter experimental station at which it is my intention to conduct a number of exhaustive tests and experiments.
>
> That this may be of some practical value to your department I am prepared to instruct an officer of the Navy in the operation and construction of the Curtiss aeroplane. As I am fully aware that the Navy department has no funds available for aviation purposes, I am making this offer with the understanding that it involves no expense for the Navy Department other than the cost of detailing an officer to the aviation grounds in Southern California. The officer so detailed would be in a position to conduct many experiments himself as well as to suggest such tests as will involve problems that the Navy department would have a special interest in solving.

The Navy quickly agreed to send one of its young officers to the Curtiss training school in California and began to examine its list of officers who had volunteered for aviation duty. On December 23, 1910, the Navy had made its selection and issued an announcement, which was published in newspapers the following day. The *New York Tribune* reported the selection on page 8 of its December 24, 1910 issue:

> The first step in the way of establishing an aeronautical corps in the Navy was taken by Assistant Secretary Winthrop to-day in detailing Lieutenant Theodore G. Ellyson to take a course in practical flying under the tutorship of Glenn Curtiss, in Los Angeles. The designation was made only after long deliberation. Candidates from nearly every branch of the service made application for the place, indicating that the Navy will never lack volunteers to take up an aerial career. The difficulty was to determine which branch was the most likely to supply the officer best qualified to become air pilot.
>
> After going over the entire list, Lieutenant Ellyson was selected because he was an expert on submarines, the nearest thing to an airship, according to the department's view, that the Navy now possesses. It is held that his experience with gasolene engines and the machinery of submarines will give him some insight into the peculiarities of an aeroplane motor, and that the cool head and steady nerve necessary for navigating a ship under water will serve him to advantage in the navigation of a ship above the water. It is not unlikely therefore, that if Mr. Ellyson achieves distinction as a naval officer it will be by sailing almost anywhere except on the bounding blue. At present he is stationed at Newport News, and has been in command of the submarine Shark. He entered the Naval Academy from Virginia.

The announcement must have been quite a nice Christmas present for Lt. Ellyson, who volunteered for aviation duty on December 16!

Naval Aviator No. 1

Born in Richmond, Virginia, in 1885, Theodore Gordon Ellyson entered the United States Naval Academy in 1901 and graduated with the class of 1905 as a midshipman. The redheaded Virginian was popular with his fellow classmen at the Academy and became a competent officer in the Navy. His promotion to lieutenant (junior grade) was held up until 1907 due to a condition of anemia, from which he recovered and was finally promoted in 1908.

During the five years following his graduation, he served on the USS *Texas* and USS *Missouri*; as Watch and Division Officer of the USS *Pennsylvania* and later USS *Colorado*; and on the USS *West Virginia*, USS *Rainbow*, and the submarine USS *Shark* on the Asiatic Station.

After his return to the United States in April 1910, he commanded the submarine USS *Tarantula* until November of that year, and then worked on the fitting out of the new submarine USS *Seal* at Newport News Shipbuilding and Drydock Company. He commanded her briefly after her commissioning on December 2, 1910. On December 16, 1910 he sent a letter to the secretary of the Navy requesting aviation duty. He was promoted to lieutenant on the day before Christmas, 1910, the same day he received orders to travel to California to be trained as an aviator at the Curtiss flying school.

Ellyson was the first United States Navy officer designated as an aviator ("Naval Aviator No.1"), and served in the experimental development of aviation in the years before and after World War I. A recipient of the Navy Cross for his aviation service in World War I, Ellyson died in 1928 when his Loening aircraft crashed into Chesapeake Bay.

Lieutenant T.G. Ellyson, Navy Air Pilot Number 1, seen here in 1912 at the controls of the Curtiss A-3 Hydroaeroplane. *Harris & Ewing Collection, Prints & Photographs Division, Library of Congress, LC-DIG-hec-01630*

Original certificates, dated January 1, 1914, designating Lieutenant Theodore Gordon Ellyson as Navy Air Pilot Number 1. The designation "Navy Air Pilot" was created by the Navy Department in 1913, and was the result of the Navy establishing the first qualification standards for those personnel assigned to flight duty. *National Naval Aviation Museum, Pensacola.*

Lt. Ellyson was ordered detached from duty as an inspector at the Newport News Shipbuilding and Dry Dock Company at Newport News, Virginia, and was told to join the Curtiss school at Los Angeles "for instruction in the art of aviation." He was further told to report his progress every month, and "when in your opinion and that of Mr. Curtiss you have qualified in practical aviation you will so report to the Navy Department."

As 1910 drew to a close, Secretary Meyer delivered his annual report to the U.S. Congress. It contained a short section on the Navy's activities in the field of aviation:

> November 14 Mr. Eugene Ely made an experiment at Hampton Roads in flying in a Curtiss biplane from the deck of the U.S.S. *Birmingham,* which had been furnished by the department. The object was to demonstrate the possibility of an aeroplane of the existing type leaving a ship for scout purposes. A temporary platform was placed forward on the *Birmingham* for the purpose of assisting the aviator with the ship's speed by steaming ahead to wind. Mr. Ely did not, however, need this help, and easily succeeded in making the flight while the ship was at anchor, thereby increasing the value of the experiment.
>
> This experiment demonstrated the conditions governing the location of future platforms on shipboard for this purpose, and showed that they could be installed without interfering seriously with the other features of the ship.
>
> Landing on or near a ship on returning with information after a scouting trip appears to be practicable.
>
> This experiment and the advances which have been made in aviation seem to demonstrate that it is destined to perform some part in the naval warfare of the future. It appears likely that this will be limited to scouting. A scout which is not strong enough to pierce the enemy's line can get as near as possible and then send an aeroplane 30 or 40 miles, obtain valuable information and then return to the scout. Even if the aviator did not land on the scout he could be brought on board and deliver his information. The loss of an aeroplane would be of no moment, as the ship may easily carry others. The distinct value of service of this kind is easily seen.
>
> The department contemplates further experiments along these lines, with the belief that it will be necessary in the near future to equip all scouts with one or more aeroplanes to increase the distance at which information can be secured.
>
> For the purpose of carrying on such experiments the department recommends that $25,000 be authorized.

To obtain authorization for the funds, Meyer testified before Congress in early January 1911 that he believed the naval airplane experiments financed by the appropriation would be of "incalculable value." Clearly Secretary Meyer's view of airplanes and airmen was changed as a result of Ely's takeoff from the *Birmingham*!

Eugene Ely's Daring Demonstration
Meanwhile, Ellyson reported to Curtiss at Los Angeles on January 2, 1911, then traveled with him to San Diego to inspect a site at North Island that had been offered to Curtiss for use as an airfield. Curtiss was pleased with the site and accepted the offer to establish his winter flying school there.

Curtiss and Ellyson then traveled north to attend the San Francisco aviation meet, primarily for the purpose of assisting Gene Ely in preparing for a daring demonstration flight that would complement his first takeoff from the deck of the *Birmingham,* i.e., to make the first landing on the deck of a ship. Even though the Navy could not afford to pay him for his attempt, Ely accepted the challenge without hesitation despite the obvious dangers involved. By some unexplained means, Chambers had arranged for the cruiser USS *Pennsylvania* to be available in San Francisco Bay, and to be modified for Ely's demonstration.

The cruiser USS *Pennsylvania,* anchored in San Francisco Bay and commanded by Captain Charles F. ("Frog") Pond, was quickly prepared for the experiment. A temporary platform was constructed over its quarterdeck that was 31 feet, 6 inches wide and 119 feet, 4 inches long – almost 50% longer than the length of the platform that had been added to the USS *Birmingham.* A ramp, 14 feet, 3 inches in length was extended directly from the end of the landing platform over the ship's stern at an angle of about 30 degrees, to prevent Ely's airplane from accidentally striking the ship's propeller.

Two metal flotation tanks were attached to Ely's airplane to keep it afloat in case Ely accidentally splashed his airplane in the water. Despite the larger dimensions of the *Pennsylvania's* landing platform, the wingspan of the fragile little Curtiss craft was only 4 feet less than the width of the platform, leaving Ely with little room for error. However, his experience on the airshow circuit provided Ely with the expertise needed for making "spot" landings. The flight was made on January 18, 1911. Ely later recounted his adventure:

> As I came out over the bay above Hunters Point, I was about 1,200 feet up. It was cloudy, smoky and hazy. I could not see the ships at first and did not locate them until I was within about two miles of them.
> I was spinning along at about 60 miles an hour with the winds directly behind me, and when I sighted the *Pennsylvania* I saw that the stern was pointed into the wind, and when about a mile away I veered off to pass over what I supposed

Ely's landing on the temporary aft deck of the USS *Pennsylvania* (Armored Cruiser #4) on January 18, 1911. Lines stretched across the deck that were anchored by sandbags acted as the arresting gear. *U.S. Naval History and Heritage Command Photograph.*

Eugene Ely on board the USS *Pennsylvania* after landing successfully. Note the hooks on the undercarriage, used for snagging the arresting cables on landing. *U.S. Naval History and Heritage Command Photograph.*

was the flagship *California*. As I neared her I dropped down from 1,000 to about 400 feet in salute to the admiral. This ship, however, proved to be the *Maryland*, as the *California* was not in the bay, and I swung around the *West Virginia*, coming down to about 100 feet above the water, and pointed my machine for the *Pennsylvania*. I then made a sharp turn about 100 yards astern of that ship, gradually dropping down.

But there was an appreciable wind blowing diagonally across the deck of the cruiser, and I had to calculate the force of this wind and the effect it would have on my approach to the landing.

I found that it was not possible to strike squarely toward the center of the landing, so I pointed the aeroplane straight toward the landing, but on a line with the windward side of the ship. I had to take the chance that I had correctly estimated just how many feet the wind would blow me out of my course.

Just as I came over the overhang at the stern, I felt a sudden lift to the machine, as I shut down the motor, caused by the breaking of the wind around the stern. This lift carried me a trifle further than I intended going before coming in actual contact with the platform.

Ely had made a safe landing! He was greeted by his wife and Captain Pond, as well as by a rousing chorus of cheers, steam whistles and sirens. After having lunch on the *Pennsylvania*, Ely flew off of its temporary platform deck at 11:58 a.m., dipped to within 10 feet of the bay's waters, and returned safely to San Francisco, where he received another wild reception.

Captain Charles F. Pond, in command of the USS *Pennsylvania* at the time, made these observations of Ely's landing:

Extract From The Report Of The Commanding Officer Of The U.S.S. "Pennsylvania," Captain C.F. Pond, U.S. N.

A special platform had previously been erected on board at the Navy Yard, Mare Island, Cal. This platform, somewhat modified from the one used by Mr. Ely in his flight from the U.S.S. *Birmingham* at Hampton Roads, Va., was 119 feet 4 inches in length, 31 feet 6 inches width in the clear, extending from the stern to the bridge-deck over the quarterdeck and after 8-inch turret, the forward end being 5 feet higher than the after end, and with a fantail of same width and 14 feet 3 inches in length sloping at an angle of about 30 degrees, over the stern. At the sides were fitted guard rails of 2-inch by 12-inch planking, and guide rails of 2-inch by 4-inch scantling, 12 feet apart, extended throughout its length. These guide rails, evidently intended to aid the aviator in determining his direction upon landing were of little or no use in that connection, but served a useful purpose in holding the lines connecting the sand bags at a proper height from the platform, though temporary blocks would have served equally as well. Every possible precaution was taken to insure the safety of the aviator. As fitted at the Navy yard, the platform bore at its forward end a canvas screen extending from the platform to the temporary searchlight platform on the mainmast underneath the lower top, intended to catch the aviator and his machine should all other means fail, and, 10 feet from its forward end, a 2-inch by 12-inch plank extending across the face of the platform. These, and especially the plank, were very crude devices, and had they come into use would probably only have caused serious if not fatal injury to the aviator and his machine. Abaft the solid plank stop and spaced about 6 feet apart were fitted two canvas screens about 20 inches in height. These, together with the slight slope of the platform, were the only means provided in the original construction to check or stop the flight of the machine. It was very evident that something more was needed and after several consultations with Messrs. Curtiss and Ely, during which several schemes were considered and rejected, it was finally decided to adopt a system of sand bags such as had been successfully used to check automobiles at racing meets. Accordingly 22 pairs of bags were placed on the platform, each bag containing 50 pounds of sand, accurately weighed to insure uniformity of action, so as not to slue the machine, each pair being connected by a 21-thread line hauled taut across the face of the platform over the guide rails. These bags, spaced about 3 feet apart, covered about 75 feet of the length of the platform. As it turned out they were ample for the purpose and worked perfectly and none of the other devices were called into play. On either side of the platform, awnings were spread, extending to the life-boat davits, to catch the aviator should he be thrown over the edge of the platform. Life preservers were supplied and expert swimmers stationed, while boats lay off on either side for use in case of necessity.

The flying machine, a Curtiss biplane, had been fitted with a central skid, its lower face about 5 inches above the plane of the wheels on which the biplane stood when at rest, to which were attached three pairs of flat steel hooks intended to catch the lines connecting the sand bags. These hooks, though simple in design, were extremely ingenious. When in position, their points, which were about 4 inches in length and with 4-inch opening, lay in a horizontal plane parallel with the face of the skid and further precaution was taken to round the extreme points so that they might not catch in the cracks of the platform. Their shanks were about 16 inches in length, and they were secured in pairs, one on either side of the skid,

by a through bolt about 5 inches from the forward end of the shank. So fitted they hung point down to the rear and projecting about 4 inches below the lower face of the skid, further depression being prevented by a wire loop and the hooks made positive in action by a spiral spring at the forward end of the shank so that they might give upon hitting any undue obstruction such as might be encountered upon rising from the ground and would immediately automatically regain their proper position. It is only necessary to add that they functioned perfectly. The machine was further fitted with two metal air tanks, one on either side and with a hydroplane forward for use in case, through accident, the landing was made in the water. There were no other special fittings, and the machine landed on its rubber-tired wheels, as upon ordinary occasions. Ely himself wore a life preserver about his shoulders improvised from the inner tube of a bicycle tire.

The flight from the aviation field at Tanforan, 10 miles distant in an air line, was made at a speed of about 60 miles an hour, as determined by the time of flight, and at an elevation of about 1500 feet. When about a half mile distant the aeroplane made a graceful dip, passing directly over the *Maryland* at an elevation of about 400 feet, then circling and continuing its descent passed over the bows of the *West Virginia* at an elevation of about 100 feet, and completing the turn at about 500 yards on our starboard quarter headed directly for the ship. When about 75 yards astern it straightened up and came on board at a speed of about 40 miles an hour, landing plumb on the center line, missing the first 11 lines attached to the sand bags – but catching the next 11, and stopping within 30 feet with 50 feet to spare, nothing damaged in the least, not a bolt or brace started, and Ely the coolest man on board. Hardly two minutes had elapsed from the time the aeroplane was first sighted, and no one had imagined he would make the landing on the first turn. The sand bags worked perfectly, stopping the machine, weighing, with the aviator, about 1000 pounds, with a speed of 40 miles an hour, within 30 feet, and, as Ely stated, with no perceptible jar. Six pairs of bags did the work, being hauled in over the guide rails close to the machine, the other five pairs being only slightly disturbed. The bags were caught, four on the first set

Eugene Ely departing the USS *Pennsylvania* after landing successfully. *Photo Courtesy of the Museum of History and Industry, Seattle, WA.*

of hooks, three on the second, and four on the third set. As the aeroplane came on board, the upward draft from the wind striking the starboard quarter of the ship lifted it bodily and gave it a slight list to port. When the size and weight of the machine, its speed of approach, the elevation from which it descended, and the effect of the wind are considered, the marvelous skill, accuracy of judgment and quickness of brain of the aviator may be imagined. The slightest error of judgment meant serious, if not fatal, injury to both the aviator and his machine. Three feet more of elevation would have forced him to plunge directly into the canvas screen, and three to ten feet less elevation would have caused him to strike the fantail with consequences which can only be surmised.

The flight from the ship, an hour later, was comparatively tame. The aeroplane took the air easily, dipping to within about 10 feet from the surface of the water and then rising to an elevation of about 2000 feet over the city. Within a very few minutes Ely was back on the aviation field, landing within 10 feet of the starting line.

Curtiss Sets a Course

Ely's shipboard landing and takeoff demonstrations were generally greeted enthusiastically, but the demonstrations had not fully satisfied the secretary of the Navy. Meyer's further requirement, as conveyed earlier to Glenn Curtiss was: "When you show me that it is feasible for an aeroplane to alight on the water alongside a battleship and be hoisted aboard without any false deck to receive it, I shall believe the airship of practical benefit to the Navy."

In the short time span of five months, the hard work and dedication of Captain Washington Irving Chambers had begun to bear fruit. But it was obvious to both Chambers and Curtiss that a completely new aircraft design was required to satisfy the Navy's aviation needs.

CHAPTER 3

Inventing the Curtiss Hydroaeroplane

Curtiss Sets up Camp in California

The demand for pilot training was growing immensely as the public became caught up in the aviation mania that was sweeping the country. The public demonstrations and contests flown by the Curtiss exhibition team in 1910 helped to provide Curtiss with the financial resources to continue the development of advanced aircraft and engines. But the profits from the public exhibitions and contests would not last forever. Curtiss had proven that he could make money selling motorcycles and engines; now he set out to make aviation a profitable venture. But first Curtiss needed to train pilots to fly the airplanes that he envisioned would grow his company.

Curtiss, whose factory and training school were located at Hammondsport, New York, searched for a winter flying ground in California because of its mild winter climate. He selected North Island, San Diego where he found all the desirable features for which he was looking. It was uninhabited (except for jack rabbits and birds); it was accessible only by boat, and thus would minimize the number of curious spectators; it experienced very nice weather; and it had a level field. It possessed beaches and access to deep water that easily allowed experiments to be performed on both the land and the water.

North Island was a flat, sandy island approximately four miles long by two miles wide with excellent beaches from which the experimental hydroplanes could be launched into the water. It was here that America's first hydroaeroplane was developed.

The Aero Club of San Diego constructed wooden sheds for the airplanes and provided landings for the small boats necessary to commute between the city and the island. Curtiss employees set up the Curtiss aviation camp in the middle of January. All hands cleared away the underbrush to provide runways, and tents were erected along the Spanish Bight estuary between North Island and Coronado.

By January 17, 1911 the Curtiss winter camp was prepared to receive the Army, Navy and civilian aviation students and to undertake aeronautical experiments. Four days later it was formally opened with exhibition flights made by Curtiss, Charles Willard, Eugene Ely and Lincoln Beachey.

Camping at North Island

In addition to Lt. Ellyson, Curtiss also had three Army officers in camp: Lt. Paul W. Beck, Lt. C.E.M. Kelly, and Lt. John C. Walker. Charles Witmer, a civilian, was also at the San Diego camp for instruction. Curtiss demonstration pilots Eugene Ely and Hugh Robinson were also in attendance, so Ellyson received flight instruction from the best Curtiss airplane pilots.

Ellyson's Naval Academy engineering training was a real asset to Curtiss. Ellyson knew machinery and he was a practical and inventive mechanic. He was determined to learn everything about aviation and not just the flying aspect. He worked on the aircraft engines so often that he could almost strip and rebuild the Curtiss engines with the same dexterity as if he were cleaning a service revolver. Mostly to provide information to Chambers back in Washington, Ellyson kept a daily log of activities. Ellyson's good attitude and willingness to get dirty allowed Curtiss to consult with him and ask for assistance in the Curtiss hydroaeroplane design experiments. The float fabrication was being accomplished by machine shops in San Diego, but Ellyson and the other students provided the muscle-power whenever Curtiss tried out his experimental "hydros."

The Curtiss students learned to fly using a unique method that had been developed by Curtiss. He had about three aircraft stationed at North Island and kept one of his 8-cylinder planes equipped with a less-powerful 4-cylinder engine. This plane was heavy and with a lower horsepower engine, was hard to get airborne. By this means, Curtiss kept his students close to the ground until he was sure they were ready to fly. To prevent "accidental" flights Curtiss also put a block of wood in the throttle pedal so that half-power was the most a student could get out of the already too-small engine.

Curtiss taught aircraft control through straight-line grasshopper-type flights, a technique called "grass-cutting." After carefully explaining the use of each control and how to use power, Curtiss and his student pilot would bounce up and down the cleared area on North Island in short hops, never more than a foot or two off the ground. Once directional control, that is, holding the plane straight, was achieved through fast taxiing, then Curtiss would move the wood block and allow a little more power to be applied and the "hopping" phase began. This forced the student to concentrate on the elevators and the control of attitude.

Because he controlled the engine horsepower, Curtiss did not have to ride along on every flight. Once the student understood the functions of the elevators, rudders, and ailerons, he was allowed to "grass-cut" by himself. Occasionally a student became accidentally airborne, but not for a long distance. Ellyson had this happen to him during his second week of training when he experienced his first crash. Ellyson and the plane were not badly hurt, but it did teach him something about "air holes" and turbulence. To avoid turbulent conditions, Curtiss' students did most of their flying in the first three hours after sunrise and during the hour before the sun went down. It meant long days for Ellyson and everyone else in camp.

Safety awareness was one of Curtiss' most important personal assets and he instilled this quality into Ellyson. Prior to every flight a careful examination of the aircraft was required. The trainees soon knew the function of every cable, carburetor, and bamboo strut. Ellyson wrote a set of instructions for pre-flighting an aircraft and later wrote a manual describing how to inspect airplanes prior to their acceptance by the Navy.

Curtiss was prepared to train as many pilots as time allowed, but he was also intent on resuming his airplane design experiments. The design of a workable seaplane for the Navy was at the top of his list of experiments. His strategy was to base the design on the successful Model D land plane or "Curtiss Standard Biplane" as it was described in the Curtiss sales catalog.

Curtiss Model D Description

The Model D was a derivative of the original Reims Racer and was being used successfully by the Curtiss exhibition team in air shows across the country. At first glance the overall lines of the diminutive biplane seemed very sparse. The spindly struts seemed too fragile to support the aircraft's wings, and the bamboo tail booms looked anachronistic. But it was classic Glenn Curtiss: every single part of the airplane had but a single function. The design philosophy of no duplicated functions resulted in a structure optimized for weight and strength.

Curtiss and the "Gold Dust Twins".

Two photos of the "Lizzie" airplane used by Curtiss for the initial ground training of student pilots at North Island, San Diego. The "Gold Dust Twins" flanking Curtiss in the top photo are (left) team pilot Charles Witmer and (right) U.S. Navy Lt. T.G. Ellyson. *Courtesy of the San Diego Air & Space Museum.*

Curtiss Model D biplane, piloted by Lt. T.G. Ellyson shown prior to his first flight at the Country Club of Coronado polo field, January 29, 1911. *Courtesy of the San Diego Air & Space Museum.*

The majority of the structure was made of laminated wood that provided the ability to absorb shocks without breaking. The landing gear was especially stout, and needed to be so because of the rough fields that the Curtiss exhibition team was encountering on their tours of the country. As we shall discuss later, the ruggedness designed into the Model D landplane would pay big dividends later in the development of the hydroaeroplane.

An important design feature of the Model D was its modular construction. The major parts of the airplane could easily be taken apart in one hour and packed into crates that were designed to easily fit into railroad boxcars. It was claimed that two experienced mechanics could reassemble the airplane in less that two hours. A side benefit of this modular design feature was the ability to quickly make repairs in case the airplane was involved in a flying accident. And the modularity of the structure allowed Curtiss the freedom to modify the airplane configuration during his hydroaeroplane experiments.

The following Model D information was taken from a Curtiss sales brochure. (Multiply the prices by 20 to get a rough idea of what the cost would be in 2011 dollars).

Model D Specifications
WIDTH – Planes, over all, 26 feet, 3 inches.
LENGTH – Front to rear control, 25 feet, 9 inches.
HEIGHTH – From ground to highest points, 7 feet 5 1/2 inches.

Description and Prices

Model D-4 – Equipped with a 4-cylinder, 40 H.P., water-cooled Curtiss motor. An excellent machine for exhibition work, endurance, etc. Speed, 45 miles per hour. Weight ready for flight, 550 pounds. Weight, packed for shipment, 950 pounds. Price, complete for shipment: $4,500

Model D-8 – Equipped with an 8-cylinder, 60 H.P., water-cooled Curtiss motor. Entire outfit identical with that used by the famous aviators of The Curtiss Exhibition Co. The safest machine, and the most suitable for a confined space. Speed 60 miles per hour. Weight, ready for flight, 650 pounds. Weight, packed for shipment, 1,000 pounds. Price, complete for shipment: $5,000

Model D-8-75 – Same as Model D, but equipped with an 8-cylinder, 75 H.P., water-cooled Curtiss motor. Capable of developing a speed of 70 miles an hour. For speed and cross-country races. Weight, ready for flight, 700 pounds. Weight, packed for shipment, 1,050 pounds. Price, complete for shipment: $5,500

Initial Twin-float Hydroaeroplane Design

Curtiss did not have time to test his new hydroaeroplane configuration before leaving for California in December 1910 so the hydro floats were shipped to California by rail. The floats were first attached to a Model D in San Diego, where water testing began in January 1911.

The simplicity of the Model D land plane became more complex when Curtiss designed his first hydroaeroplane version of the land plane. The main component of the hydroaeroplane design was a wide and relatively short main float, located directly under the lower wing. The design of this float was similar to the float that Henri Fabre had used on his *hydravion*. A small float mounted on booms forward of the wings provided balance for the aircraft on water.

Curtiss recalled the early development stages of his hydroaeroplane in the April 1912 issue of the *Aero Club of America Bulletin*:

> My first idea of an aeroplane was one built to start and alight on the ice. This appealed to me because a frozen lake presented an ideal aviation field on account of being free from obstructions, smooth and level. It proved comparatively easy to build a machine to rise from the ice. This was done first at Hammondsport when the *Red Wing* made its flight from the frozen surface of Lake Keuka in 1908. The following summer we tried to rise from the water but found it, as we expected, much more difficult.
>
> Our first experiments (with the *Loon*) were with two pontoons in the form of a catamaran. We afterward tried a single boat (the "Canoe Machine") and decided that this would be the ultimate type. Bad weather came on in the fall and the experiments were discontinued.
>
> The summer following, 1909, my time was taken up in building a Gordon Bennett racer and perfecting the regular land machines. During 1910, I was so busy with exhibition work that I did not get a chance to do anything more with the hydro, although I had hoped to have one completed for the Albany to New York flight. I was obliged to undertake this, however, with a regular machine fitted with inflated rubber tubes for flotation in case of alighting on the water and a device for alighting safely on the surface of the water and to prevent the machine from turning over.
>
> So that it was the winter of 1910 in San Diego, Cal., when I found an opportunity to experiment further on the hydroaeroplane. My first device was somewhat of a freak and our greatest trouble at first was to prevent the propeller

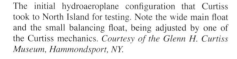

The initial hydroaeroplane configuration that Curtiss took to North Island for testing. Note the wide main float and the small balancing float, being adjusted by one of the Curtiss mechanics. *Courtesy of the Glenn H. Curtiss Museum, Hammondsport, NY.*

from being broken by striking the spray from the boat. This we endeavored to accomplish by using a very wide float in the rear so that all of the spray would pass outside of the propeller. This float was made of a form to present the least resistance to the air and also to be somewhat of a lifting surface. It was fairly satisfactory in smooth water but gave us much trouble in a rough sea.

Top: The final variant of Curtiss' initial hydroaeroplane configuration being readied for testing. A large planing surface has been added, placed 5 to 6 ft. in front of the small balancing float. *Courtesy of the San Diego Air & Space Museum.*

Above: The final variant of Curtiss' initial hydroaeroplane configuration, shown during low speed water testing. Curtiss managed to get this machine airborne for a short distance on January 26, 1911. *Courtesy of the San Diego Air & Space Museum.*

The first taxi tests on water revealed a design flaw that became very difficult to completely fix. The basic problem was that the thrust line of the engine was so far above the water line that, upon application of takeoff power, the front float plowed through the water rather than floating on top of the water. The additional water drag made it impossible to achieve liftoff speed.

Several modifications were made to keep the front float from plowing through the water, but each succeeding fix added more complexity to an already complex-looking aircraft. The accompanying series of figures show some of the major modifications that were made to the aircraft to improve its handling in water.

One day in late January 1911 Curtiss finally managed to lift the ungainly aircraft a few feet into the air, but he was not happy with its flying qualities or its handling on water. He made a few more short hops that day and then retired to his rented home in Coronado where he sketched a new and simplified design with a single pontoon that replaced the majority of the complicated devices on the test aircraft.

Single-float Design and U.S. Patents

Curtiss described his thoughts about improving his first hydroaeroplane design:

> It was then evident that a long boat (pontoon) must be used to ride through the waves and that it must extend well forward and be shaped in such a manner that it would always tend to rise on the surface, even though waves washed over its deck.

The Baker Machine Company of San Diego constructed the new wooden pontoon using thin spruce for the covering and Curtiss made the first flight using the new pontoon on January 26, 1911. The aircraft-pontoon combination was a complete

The first single-float design that provided the basis for all of the following Curtiss hydroaeroplane designs. The float greatly simplified the aircraft configuration and provided easier takeoffs and landings on water. Note the spray deflector board on top of the float. *Courtesy of the Glenn H. Curtiss Museum, Hammondsport, NY.*

success compared with the original design. On January 26 Curtiss flew the aircraft several hundred feet above the harbor, serenaded by many ships' whistles. The world's first practical hydroaeroplane had successfully flown! But the new design still required some improvements and Curtiss continued to tinker with the design.

Lt. Ellyson's chapter in the *Curtiss Aviation Book* gives us a glimpse of the work ethic that Curtiss exhibited during the experimental phase of the hydro development:

> What is not generally known is the hard work and the many disappointments encountered before the hydroaeroplane was a real success. Mr. Curtiss had two objects in view: first, the development of the hydroaeroplane, and secondly, the personal instruction of his pupils. The latter was accomplished early in the morning and late in the afternoon as these were the only times when the wind conditions were suitable, and the experimental work was carried on during the rest of the day, and, I think, Mr. Curtiss also worked the best part of the remainder of the time, as I well remember one important change that was made as the result of an idea that occurred to him while he was shaving. No less than fifty changes were made from the original idea, and those of us who did not then know Mr. Curtiss well, wondered that he did not give up in despair. Since that time we have learned that anything that he says he can do, he always accomplishes, as he always works the problem out in his mind before making any statement.

> All of us who were learning to fly were also interested in the construction of the machines, and when not running "Lizzy" (our practice machine) up and down the field, felt honored at being allowed to help work on the experimental machine. You see it was not Curtiss, the genius and inventor, whom we knew.

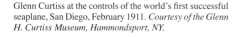

Glenn Curtiss at the controls of the world's first successful seaplane, San Diego, February 1911. *Courtesy of the Glenn H. Curtiss Museum, Hammondsport, NY.*

It was 'G.H.,' a comrade and chum, who made us feel that we were all working together, and that our ideas and advice were really of some value. It was never a case of "do this" or "do that," to his amateur or to his regular mechanics, but always, 'What do you think of making this change?' He was always willing to listen to any argument but generally managed to convince you that his plan was the best. I could write volumes on Curtiss, the man, but fear that I am wandering from the subject in hand.

One of the results of the experiments at San Diego was to show that such a hydroaeroplane, or a development of it, was thoroughly suitable for naval use. Although it was the first of May before Mr. Curtiss returned to his factory at Hammondsport, specifications, which were approximately as follows, were sent him and he was asked if he could make delivery by the first of July: "A hydroaeroplane, capable of rising from or landing on either the land or the water, capable of attaining a speed of at least fifty-five miles an hour, with a fuel supply for four hours' flight. To carry two people and be so fitted that either person could control the machine."

Curtiss taxiing his hydroaeroplane prior to taking off on a test flight over the waters of San Diego Bay. *Courtesy of the Glenn H. Curtiss Museum, Hammondsport, NY.*

Floating toward his base at North Island after a successful test hop, Curtiss waits for his crew to wade out and help him bring the aircraft onto the beach. *Courtesy of the Glenn H. Curtiss Museum, Hammondsport, NY.*

aircraft was in the water alongside a ship. A sailor could more easily crank the propeller to start the engine if it was in the front of the airplane rather than behind the wings.

Therefore Curtiss rotated the engine 180 degrees and thus made a tractor version out of his standard pusher design. The pilot's seat was placed aft of the engine to achieve a balanced configuration. The aircraft was assembled fairly quickly to take advantage of an opportunity to demonstrate the hydroaeroplane to the Navy.

The USS *Pennsylvania*, under the command of Captain Pond, had sailed from San Francisco and was anchored in San Diego harbor. On February 17, Curtiss was invited by Pond to fly over to the *Pennsylvania* and "come aboard." After hurriedly readying the aircraft for the flight, Curtiss attempted to take off but quickly discovered that the aircraft was nose heavy. Apparently there had been little time to prepare for the flight and Curtiss' crew had not properly balanced the airplane. He made one more attempt at a takeoff and briefly flew a few feet above the harbor before landing and then taxiing the remainder of the distance to the awaiting *Pennsylvania*.

A cable and a hook, deployed from one of the ship's boat cranes was lowered to fetch Curtiss and his aircraft from the water. Curtiss attached the hook to his aircraft, but not trusting the safety of the attachment, rode up to the deck on the hook and cable. Once Curtiss and the aircraft were aboard ship, Captain Pond greeted him, and a short time later Curtiss and his aircraft were lowered to the water. Ellyson was in a small boat, waiting to help Curtiss maneuver the aircraft away from the ship and

Below: The tractor version of the hydroaeroplane was designed to permit open-water starting of the engine by Navy crewmen standing on the pontoon. In these photos Curtiss demonstrates the pilot's position behind the engine and the tractor propeller location. *Courtesy of the Glenn H. Curtiss Museum, Hammondsport, NY.*

Bottom: The hydroaeroplane tractor version, shown on February 17, 1911. Curtiss is shown preparing to fly to the USS *Pennsylvania* to be hoisted aboard the ship. *Courtesy of the Glenn H. Curtiss Museum, Hammondsport, NY.*

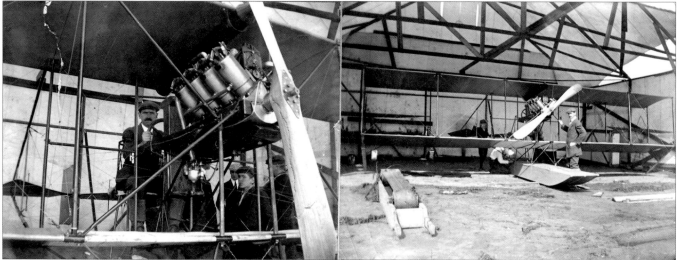

Curtiss and the tractor hydroaeroplane being hoisted aboard the USS *Pennsylvania*, anchored in San Diego Bay, February 17, 1911. Not trusting the attachment to the airplane's wing, Curtiss rode up on the hoist's hook. *Courtesy of the Glenn H. Curtiss Museum, Hammondsport, NY.*

also to start the engine. Curtiss taxied the aircraft back to his camp at high speed and the tractor version never flew again.

Several aspects of the tractor hydroaeroplane made it a non-starter as far as Curtiss was concerned. The engine sprayed oil over the pilot, who had limited forward vision, and the propeller blast was very uncomfortable for the pilot. Nonetheless, Curtiss had successfully demonstrated the aircraft's capability of deployment from a ship using only the ship's existing equipment. It was evident that Secretary Meyer's single requirement had been satisfied, that is, Curtiss had shown that it was "feasible for an aeroplane to alight on the water alongside a battleship and be hoisted aboard without any false deck to receive it."

The World's First Amphibious Aircraft
Curtiss developed the hydroaeroplane from the landplane by substituting pontoons for the wheeled landing gear. It became obvious to him that an aircraft that could operate both on land and in the water would enhance the marketability of the hydroaeroplane.

Using the single-float design as a basis, Curtiss placed retractable wheels on each side of the main pontoon and added a small nosewheel under the bow of the pontoon. Named the "*Triad*," it was successfully flown at North Island on February 26, 1911, a month after the first successful flight of the hydroaeroplane. The flight that day began on the water and after a brief landing on a nearby sandspit, Curtiss taxied back into the water, took off again and then landed on the beach near the Hotel del Coronado. Later in the afternoon, he took off from the beach and landed in the water close to the Curtiss camp. The amphibian as we know it today had first flown that day, the product of the inventive genius of Glenn Curtiss.

The military implications of a single aircraft's ability to operate from land or water were apparent to Curtiss. He wrote the following in the autobiographical work, *The Curtiss Aviation Book,* published in 1912:

> With these achievements it seems to me the aeroplane has reached the point of utility for military purposes, either for the Army or Navy. It now seems possible to use it to establish communication between the Navy and Army, when there are no other means of communication. That is, a warship could launch an

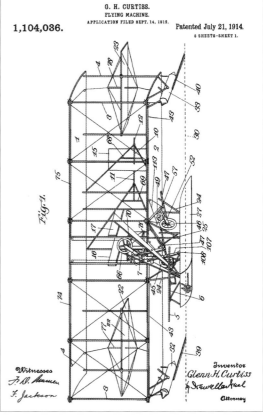

aeroplane that can fly over sea and land and come to earth on whichever element affords the best landing. Having fulfilled its mission on shore it could start from the land, and, returning to the home ship, land at its side and be picked up, as I was picked up and hoisted aboard the *Pennsylvania* at San Diego.

The Navy's interest in the *Triad* undoubtedly arose from the desire to provide the Marines with an aircraft that would be an adjunct to their warfighting role on shore. Captain Chambers, in particular, was very supportive of the amphibian concept and he later influenced the design of the Curtiss "OWL" (Over Water and Land). The OWL is described in detail in the following chapter.

In 1914 Curtiss was awarded U.S. patent number 1,104,036 for the *Triad* hydroaeroplane configuration. The patent is titled "Flying Machine." It was followed in 1915 by U.S. patent number 1,156,215 and in 1916 by U.S. patent number 1,203,550. Finally, in 1922 the U.S. patent number 1,420,609 was issued for a "Hydroaeroplane."

Having successfully proven the usefulness of his aircraft designs to the Navy, Curtiss prepared to receive an aircraft order from Washington.

Right: "Flying Machine," U.S. patent 1,104,036, the first of several patents awarded to Glenn Curtiss for the hydroaeroplane and its unique features. *US Patent Office Image.*

Below: An experimental version of the *Triad*, with its nose wheel and front elevator removed. *Courtesy of the Glenn H. Curtiss Museum, Hammondsport, NY.*

The Navy Orders Two Curtiss Aircraft

While Curtiss was busy proving the value of his aircraft for naval operations, Congress was debating the need to spend money on naval aircraft. The funding request from Secretary Meyer was finally approved and the Naval Appropriations Act of March 4, 1911 included $25,000 for naval aviation. The Act allocated all of the funds to the Bureau of Navigation, where naval aviation activities were managed over the next three years.

On May 8, 1911 the Navy Department placed an order for two Curtiss aircraft, one hydroaeroplane convertible to land type, later designated the A-l; and one land type, with four-cylinder engine, designated the A-2. The May 8 order has been officially designated as the birth date of U.S. Naval Aviation.

In addition, the Navy placed an order for one aircraft, the B-1, from the Wright brothers.

The Navy requisition orders were split between the Steam Engineering Bureau, which ordered the engines and the Navigation Bureau, which ordered the airframes. The Steam Engineering Bureau order for both engines was No. 113 (1911) and the Navigation Bureau orders were Nos. 1 and 3 (1912) for the two airframes. The engine requisition order was presumably effective in 1911 but the Navigation Bureau requisition was made effective for FY1912. Chambers would later learn that the Navy could not accept the aircraft until July 1 because the funds were not available until July 1, the start of the fiscal year. (The FY in those years ran between July 1 and June 30).

The contractual delivery dates for the A-1 and A-2 were set at July 13 and July 24, respectively. The aircraft were to be delivered to Annapolis, MD, where a new naval air training facility was being built.

Specifications for the A-l were as follows:

> One Curtiss eight cylinder biplane or "Triad" fitted for rising from or alighting on land or water, including land equipment, water equipment, and combination equipment, fitted with engine panels and chassis and four other interchangeable wing panels, covered with rubberized linen on top and tight woven special sail cloth on the bottom. One main pontoon and pair of balancing hydroplanes, with pontoons and hydro-surface to enable the machine to float when alighting on the water with land equipment attached.

> Landing wheels with suitable rims and clincher tires, capable of being housed above or extended beneath the line of the main pontoon by the aviator during flight. Subject to alterations if approved by the Naval Inspector at the factory. All complete with metal tipped propeller designed for a speed of at least forty-five miles per hour. The same to be fitted with a capacity for one passenger seated alongside the pilot and with double controls so that either the pilot or the passenger may operate the machine.

> In addition thereto, the following spare parts: one complete aileron, one complete front control, one pair diagonal braces, one rear wheel with tire, four complete sections of surfaces, two wing tip skids, 100 feet 1/16" cable, 50 feet 1/32" cable, one dozen 3/8" bolts and nuts, one dozen 5/16" bolts and nuts, one dozen 1/4" bolts and nuts, four frame sockets, four vertical posts, two propellers, one aviator's seat, one steering wheel, one complete main pontoon, four bamboos, and one strap suitably prepared for use in hoisting on board ship. The above to be furnished complete for operation, suitably boxed and delivered to the General Storekeeper, U.S. Naval Academy, Annapolis, Maryland, on or about July, 1, 1911.

By late April the weather in New York was good enough for Curtiss to begin to move his school and experimental work back to Hammondsport. Ellyson was a bit concerned about his own flight training. In San Diego Curtiss was using the one 8-

cylinder model exclusively for his experiments therefore Ellyson had to do his flying using the 4-cylinder model.

At Curtiss' suggestion, Ellyson asked Chambers if he could go to Hammondsport with Curtiss when he closed the camp in San Diego. Ellyson could then more properly study the construction of aircraft and aero engines at the Curtiss factory. He also reasoned that he could get full instruction in the hydroaeroplane, and other experimental 8-cylinder models as they were produced. Chambers wanted Ellyson close to him to ask for advice on beginning a training camp near Annapolis and consequently agreed to Ellyson's proposal.

In Hammondsport, Curtiss continued to refine the hydroaeroplane that he had successfully flown in San Diego. The Navy's specification would be hard to meet using the Model D hydroaeroplane, so Curtiss decided that a larger, more robust aircraft needed to be designed to be acceptable to the Navy. Curtiss named the new aircraft the Model E.

Curtiss A-1 - The Navy's First Airplane
The following specifications for the Model E are from the 1912 Curtiss sales catalog:

Model E Specifications
WIDTH – Planes, over all, 28 feet, 8 inches.
LENGTH – Front to rear control, 25 feet, 9 inches.
HEIGHTH – From ground to highest point, 8 feet.

Description and Prices

Model E-4 – Equipped with a 4-cyl motor, 40 H.P. water-cooled Curtiss motor. This machine is a slow, strong flying aeroplane, especially suitable for aviation schools and beginners. It is also available for high, dry altitudes. Speed, 40 miles per hour. Weight, ready for flight, 600 pounds. Weight, packed for shipment, 1000 pounds. Price, complete for shipment: $4,500

Model E-8 – Equipped with an 8-cylinder, 60 H.P. water-cooled Curtiss motor. A machine that combines speed with the advantages of weight carrying. Equipped with the Curtiss alternating dual control system. A machine that makes aviation a sport. Speed, 55 miles per hour. Weight, ready for flight, 700 pounds. Weight, packed for shipment, 1050 pounds. Price, complete for shipment: $5,000

Model E-8-75 – The same as model E-8, but equipped with an 8-cylinder, 75 H.P. Curtiss motor. The surplus power gives greater speed as well as more weight-carrying possibilities. Speed, 60 miles per hour. Weight, ready for flight, 750 pounds. Weight, packed for shipment, 1,100 pounds. Price, complete for shipment: $5,500

After the prototype Model E was fitted with the pontoon that had been developed in San Diego, Curtiss began testing the aircraft on Lake Keuka. On one test flight Curtiss had unknowingly taken off with a substantial amount of water in the pontoon and as he pointed the nose of the aircraft down to descend, the water ran forward to the front of the pontoon. The aircraft became so nose heavy that Curtiss was unable to pull the nose up. When the aircraft crashed into the lake, Curtiss was thrown out of his seat and into the forward elevator and outriggers, causing him to suffer several cuts and bruises. After that incident, the forward elevator was moved to a much lower position, only a few inches above the pontoon and below the level of the pilot's feet.

Meanwhile work continued on the Navy's A-1 and A-2 at the factory in Hammondsport in anticipation of a mid-1911 delivery to the Navy. Ellyson learned to fly Curtiss' Model E hydroaeroplane and he acted as the Navy's factory inspector for the A-1 and A-2. Curtiss sketched most of the airplane parts on whitewashed walls within the factory buildings at Hammondsport. This system seemed to work very well because Curtiss could quickly show the mechanics how to make the parts and how to fit them together to form major parts of the airplanes. However, one night a newly hired janitor whitewashed over Curtiss' sketches and the parts had to be re-drawn from memory by Curtiss. This resulted in a two-week delay in production.

The A-1 *Triad* was originally equipped with a 50 hp 8-cylinder engine but it was upgraded with a 75-hp 8-cylinder engine after the first few test flights.

The A-2 was designed to be a single-seat training aircraft for the A-1, and as such it was ordered with a small, 50 hp 4-cylinder engine.

Opposite
Top: Lieutenant T.G. Ellyson with Captain W.I. Chambers as a passenger in a Curtiss hydroaeroplane at Hammondsport, New York in 1911. *U.S. Naval History and Heritage Command Photograph.*

Bottom: Lt. T.G. Ellyson and a passenger preparing to flight test the A-1 on Lake Keuka with the *Triad* landing gear attached, summer, 1911. *Courtesy of the Glenn H. Curtiss Museum, Hammondsport, NY.*

Above: This group photo commemorates the delivery of the U.S. Navy's first airplane, the Curtiss A-1. Shown at Hammondsport, NY on July 1, 1911, are Glenn Curtiss, Capt. W.I. Chambers, Lt. J.H. Towers, Lt. T.G. Ellyson, and Curtiss publicity agent W.H. Pickens. *Courtesy of the Glenn H. Curtiss Museum, Hammondsport, NY.*

Below: The Navy's second airplane, the Curtiss A-2, shown at Hammondsport, NY with tin floats to provide flotation in case of an emergency landing in nearby Lake Keuka. *Courtesy of the Glenn H. Curtiss Museum, Hammondsport, NY.*

Below: Curtiss A-2 at Hammondsport with 8-cylinder engine installed to permit two-crew operation. *U.S. Naval History and Heritage Command Photograph.*

Bottom: Navy Lt. T.G. Ellyson in command of the Curtiss A-2 at Hammondsport, NY, August 1911. His copilot is Navy Lt. J.H. Towers. *U.S. Naval History and Heritage Command Photograph.*

Because the Navy would soon receive two aircraft, Chambers realized that another Navy pilot would need to be trained. The man selected was Lt. (j.g.) John H. Towers, who had volunteered for naval aviation duty in November 1910. Towers reported to Hammondsport on June 27, 1911 and immediately began assisting Ellyson. Ellyson trained Towers to fly using the same techniques that he had been taught by Curtiss in San Diego.

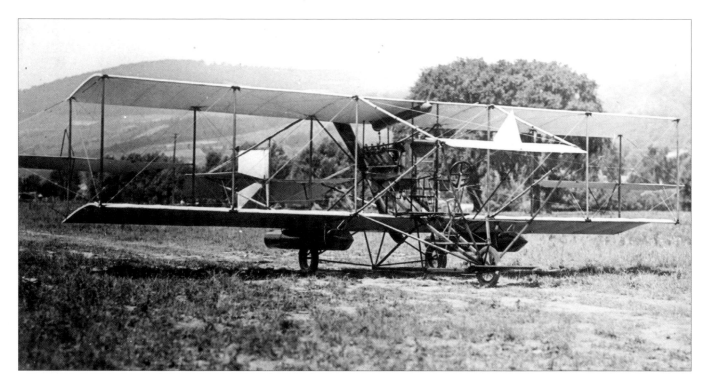

John H. Towers

A native of Rome, Georgia, Towers graduated from the United States Naval Academy in 1906 and then went to sea, serving with distinction aboard the battleship USS *Kentucky*.

He became interested in aviation and after numerous requests for aviation duty he was finally granted his wish and assigned to the Curtiss Flying School on June 27, 1911. There he became Naval Aviator No.3, following Theodore Ellyson and John Rodgers.

In December 1912 he completed flight tests that demonstrated the ability to spot submarines from the air, even in the muddy waters of the Chesapeake Bay. In 1913 he was in charge of the aviation unit that began its first operations with the fleet off Guantanamo Bay, Cuba. He and his fellow Navy pilots explored all the potential uses of their aircraft including aerial reconnaissance, bombing, aerial photography, and wireless communications.

In January 1914 he set up the first training Naval Air Station in an abandoned Navy yard at Pensacola, Florida. It was from here that he led his unit in the first Naval air operations during the Mexican crisis.

After World War I he participated in one of the greatest exploits in aviation history. In 1919 he led the Navy's trans-Atlantic flight of Curtiss NC flying boats. When they took off on May 8 on the historic flight, he was in command of the flight and of the NC-3. Flying through rainsqualls and fog, his NC-3 became lost and he had to land on the ocean. Unable to take off again because of buckled wing struts, he turned to his experience as a seaman. Rigging a canvas bucket for a sea anchor he used the aircraft's rudder to drift sail toward the Azores, 200 miles away. It was an almost impossible task, but fifty-two grueling hours later he and his crew taxied their battered aircraft into harbor in the Azores. Nine days later the NC-4 flew on to Lisbon to complete the historic first trans-Atlantic flight.

But perhaps his greatest contribution was his vision in 1921, when he began training Navy pilots in land planes, in anticipation of the Navy's commitment to aircraft carriers. In 1922 the Navy converted a collier into the USS *Langley*, the first aircraft carrier, and the practical problems of operating aircraft from it were gradually solved. The carriers *Lexington* and *Saratoga* were also authorized and these three ships eventually became the nucleus of the pre-war carrier fleet. Towers served as Executive Officer and later, Commander of the USS *Langley* and also later of the USS *Saratoga*.

In June, 1939, he became Chief of the Bureau of Aeronautics, with the rank of Admiral, becoming the first pioneer Naval aviator to achieve flag rank, and was responsible for expanding Naval aviation in those days of ever-changing criteria.

By 1943 a tremendous change was evident in the Pacific war as the "Flat-Top" became "Queen" of the fleet and its aircraft led the fleet toward victory in the world's greatest sea-borne Air Force.

At the end of the war, he commanded the second Carrier Task Force, Task Force 38, and the Fifth Fleet.

He then served as the Commander in Chief of the Pacific Fleet and finally as Chief of the Navy's General Board. In 1947 he ended a long and distinguished forty-one-year career in Naval aviation. Towers died in 1955.

Lieutenants John H. Towers and Theodore G. Ellyson, Naval Aviators numbers 3 and 1, respectively. *Courtesy of the San Diego Air & Space Museum.*

Acceptance testing of the A-1 and A-2 at Hammondsport

Curtiss made the first flight of the A-1 *Triad* on July 1, 1911. The flight began at 6:50 p.m. and lasted 5 minutes. A Curtiss 50-hp 8-cylinder engine powered the aircraft. All indications are that the flight was a success because 5 minutes later Curtiss took Ellyson up for another flight of 5 minutes and let him handle the controls. Five minutes later Ellyson soloed in the A-1 on a 15-minute flight over Lake Keuka, followed by a final 12-minute fight that began at 7:40 p.m.

The following evening 5 flights were conducted, 2 solo flights by Ellyson and 3 piloted by Curtiss with Capt. Chambers as a passenger on one of the flights. The next day Ellyson, with Chambers as a passenger attempted to fly the length of Lake Keuka, but the A-1 was not able to lift off the water so the trip was made entirely on the water surface. The 50-hp engine proved to be too marginal for flying the aircraft with two people aboard.

Right: The Curtiss Model O eight cylinder engine, forerunner of the OX-5 engine. *Courtesy of the Montana Historical Society Research Center-Photograph Archives, Helena, Montana, Photo PAC 79-36.305.*

Below: Glenn Curtiss is shown accelerating in the A-1 *Triad* for a takeoff from the surface of Lake Keuka. Curtiss is leaning to his right, thereby deflecting the ailerons to counteract the torque of the propeller. *U.S. Naval History and Heritage Command Photograph.*

The new 75-hp engine was being tested concurrently by Curtiss and it was installed on the A-1 on July 7 and test-flown by Curtiss. Finding the performance satisfactory, Curtiss and Ellyson made a flight that evening and reported "with two passengers it rose quickly with engine open."

On July 10 Curtiss took off from land, retracted the *Triad*'s landing gear and landed on Lake Keuka. One of the landing gear forks was bent during takeoff, so on July 12 the *Triad* landing gear and main float were replaced with a landplane chassis. At the same time, two large pontoons fabricated from tin were attached to the lower wing to provide a measure of safety in case the aircraft had to make a forced landing in water. In this configuration Ellyson continued flying from land, giving rides to Towers and several of Curtiss' employees. It is doubtful that the A-1 ever flew again in the *Triad* configuration.

The 75-hp Model O motor was a constant source of trouble during the early flights. The main bearings had to be replaced several times. Broken cylinders, oil leaks, fouled spark plugs, leaking radiator, loose wires and many other problems vexed the Curtiss mechanics. The engine was finally removed from the A-1 in late July and was completely rebuilt. No flights were made for over one month while the engine problems were diagnosed and repaired.

The Model O engine problems were eventually fixed and the engine went through further development to emerge as the famous and reliable OX-5 engine, of which thousands were produced in World War I.

The A-2 made its first flight on July 13 with Glenn Curtiss at the controls. Towers and Ellyson alternated as pilots on the A-2 for the remainder of July. During the time of the A-1 engine problems, flying the A-2 provided valuable training experience for Towers and Ellyson.

The new Navy training facility at Greenbury Point, near Annapolis, had not been completed by the time the two Navy aircraft had been completed. Therefore, on July 13, Ellyson sent the following letter to the Chief of the Bureau of Navigation requesting that delivery be made in Hammondsport, rather than Annapolis:

1. I request that I be authorized to accept, immediately, the two Curtiss aeroplanes contracted for by the Bureau of navigation, and the two Curtiss engines contracted for by the Bureau of Steam Engineering, dates of delivery at Annapolis, Md., July 13th and 24th, respectively, with a written agreement that The Curtiss Aeroplane Co. deliver the above articles at Annapolis, Md., at such time as the Department may direct, express charges prepaid. The delivery on the above articles has been delayed at my request awaiting the Department's reply.

2. I have been informed that the aerodrome at Annapolis is not at present in condition for practice work or for the proper care of the machines. Mr. Curtiss has offered me the use of two sheds for the use of the Navy machines and requested that practice be continued here until such time as the aerodrome at Annapolis was ready for use, and has offered the use of his shops. The machines have been tested as stated below, found most satisfactory in all respects.

3. I have made 41 flights in the 8-cylinder machine, time in air 9 1/2 hours, engine run 13 1/2 hours including block tests. Longest block test 2 hours, showing gasoline consumption of 4.7 gals. per hour at a thrust of 370 pounds. Greatest thrust on 10 minute test 520 lbs. Nine of these flights were made with a passenger, the longest of these flights being of 30 minutes duration, throttle wide open, over 16 mile course, speed 61 miles per hour. The machine has been tested as follows; *Triad*, rising from land and landing on the water, then rising from the water and landing on the land. Hydroplane, boat pontoon chassis and balancing pontoons on the wings. Land rig consisting of the wheel chassis only. And land rig with hydro surface in front and pontoons under the planes so that

it could be landed on either the land or the water, but impossible to rise from the water. The object of the latter rig is to enable the machine to be flown over either land or water with safety, and at the same time increase the speed of the machine ten miles an hour, over the *Triad* rig.

4. In view of the fact that the machines have passed all tests satisfactory I request that I be authorized to accept the machines immediately, in order that I may carry on further practice here.

Ellyson's request slowly made its way through the bureaus and was finally approved on August 10. Meanwhile, flying at Hammondsport continued at a steady pace.

Flying the A-1 resumed on August 30 with Ellyson and Towers on board. A magneto spark wire broke and the engine stopped, resulting in a forced landing on Lake Keuka where the plane capsized. Apparently the tin floats provided enough buoyancy for the aircraft to be towed to shore. Ellyson and Towers were not hurt in the accident.

The A-1 was repaired and the hydro float re-installed. Testing on water resumed on September 2 when another accident occurred. While turning on the water, the propeller struck the surface of the water and separated from its hub in two pieces, causing major damage to the aircraft structure. However, the A-1 was again quickly repaired and resumed flying two days later.

Cable Launch Experiment

On September 7 Ellyson performed a feat of airmanship that has never been repeated. Ellyson had long pondered the problem of launching a hydroaeroplane from a ship and had come up with the idea of launching by means of sliding down a cable rigged high above a ship's deck. A launch in that manner would presumably have interfered very little with the warfighting duties of the ship. It would avoid the problem of stopping the ship to launch the aircraft, or a launching from a special deck built over the ship's guns.

To test the somewhat risky maneuver, a land-based setup for the cable launch was constructed at Hammondsport. A platform sixteen feet high was erected close to the shore of Lake Keuka and a cable two hundred and fifty feet long was stretched from

Below: Setting up the A-1 for the cable-launch experiment at Hammondsport, NY, September 1911. A shallow channel has been attached to the bottom of the float to guide the airplane down the cable. Two smaller cables support the wings. *Courtesy of the Glenn H. Curtiss Museum, Hammondsport, NY.*

Opposite
Top: The Curtiss A-1 resting on the experimental launch cables prior to being winched up to the launch tower. *Courtesy of the Glenn H. Curtiss Museum, Hammondsport, NY.*

Bottom: Lt. T.G. Ellyson at the controls of the A-1 on the experimental cable launch tower. Lt. J.H. Towers is holding the line on the left and Augustus Post is standing below the A-1, holding another line. *Courtesy of the Glenn H. Curtiss Museum, Hammondsport, NY.*

the platform to an underwater piling in the lake. One of Curtiss' hydroaeroplanes was set on the cable near the platform on which men stood to crank the propeller. A groove was made along the bottom of the central float in which the cable fitted loosely, to guide it as it slid down, until sufficient speed was obtained to enable the wings of the aeroplane to support the weight of the machine.

Lt. T.G. Ellyson flying the A-1 off the cables and out over Lake Keuka in a successful experimental using a cable launch device, September 7, 1911. *Courtesy of the Glenn H. Curtiss Museum, Hammondsport, NY.*

The following is Ellyson's description of the test:

> The engine was started and run at full speed, and then I gave the signal to release the machine. The machine gained headway so rapidly that the people holding the ropes could not have used them even if there had been any necessity, but the balance was under perfect control from the start. I held the machine on the wire as long as possible, as I wanted to be sure that I had enough headway to rise and not run the risk of the machine partly rising and then falling back on the wire outside the groove. Everything happened so quickly and went off so smoothly that I hardly knew what happened except that I did have the use of the ailerons and that the machine was sensitive to their action.

Chambers' initial reaction to the successful test was enthusiastic but after thinking more about the impracticability of the cable arrangement aboard a ship, he decided to abandon the concept and instead focused on building a compressed-air catapult based on an old torpedo tube.

Annapolis Overture

By early September the Navy training camp at Annapolis had been established and was ready to receive the two Curtiss airplanes and a Wright airplane that John Rodgers had been testing. In September all three officers received orders to report to the Superintendent of the Naval Academy and to Captain Thomas Kinkaid, the officer in charge of the Naval Academy Engineering Experimental Station.

During the summer of 1911 a flying field had been established at Greenbury Point, located across the Severn River from the Academy and adjacent to the Academy's rifle range. A hangar was built with 3 bays to house the A-1, A-2, and the Wright B-1. Curtiss shipped the A-1 and A-2 to Annapolis on September 17 and flying commenced at Greenbury Point on September 30, 1911.

In the short time span of only one year, Captain Chambers had been looking after aviation affairs for the Navy and during that period several key events occurred that established a solid foundation for the expansion of U.S. Naval aviation. Most of all, Chambers deserves the credit for selecting Glenn Curtiss and his company to design, build and test the Navy's first aircraft. Without Curtiss and his dedicated team of pilots, mechanics and engineers, the enthusiastic young Navy officers would not have been able to advance the effectiveness of U.S. Naval aviation.

It was now the responsibility of those young officers to train other officers to fly and to develop their aircraft into effective weapons of war for the Navy.

CHAPTER 4

The Hydroaeroplane in Service
with the World's Navies

The U.S. Navy's purchase of the Curtiss Hydroaeroplane, combined with the Curtiss Exhibition Company's promotion of its products, resulted in the sale of the Hydro to several of the world's navies. Many of the Hydro's military operations are well documented, but some have received very little exposure. As far as is known, the Hydro served with military units in the following countries: United States of America, Russia, Italy, Japan, and Germany.

United States of America

The Curtiss Hydroaeroplane served in the U.S. Navy, the U.S. Marine Corps, and the U.S. Army. There are ambiguous references to the Hydro having served in the Naval Militias of a few states, but no definitive evidence has been found. The period of service was very short, beginning in 1911 with the Navy's introduction into service of the A-1 and A-2. The Hydro was phased out in late 1916, being replaced by more modern and perhaps safer airplanes. Some of the Hydros were retained for a few more years to conduct experimental testing of pontoons and other equipment, but the Hydro's service life was basically over by late 1916.

The Navy purchased 14 Curtiss Hydros in the years 1911 through 1916, with the majority of the airplanes delivered from 1914 through 1916. The Navy also purchased a few hydroaeroplanes from Wright and from Burgess. The list of Curtiss Navy Hydros, in the order of their entry into service is as follows:

A-1 - 1911
A-2 (converted to an E-1, then re-designated AX-1) - 1911
A-3 (re-designated AH-3 in 1914) - 1912
A-4 (re-designated AH-2 in 1914) - 1914
AH-8 - 1914
AH-9 - 1914
AH-11 - 1915
AH-12 - 1915
AH-13 - 1915
AH-14 - 1915
AH-15 - 1915
AH-16 - 1916
AH-17 - 1916
AH-18 - 1916

The First 20 Naval Aviators

1	ELLYSON, Theodore G., USN
2	RODGERS, John, USN
3	TOWERS, John H., USN
4	HERBSTER, Victor D., USN
5	CUNNINGHAM, Alfred A., USMC
6	SMITH, Bernard L., USMC
7	CHEVALIER, Godfrey deC., USN
8	BELLINGER, Patrick N. L., USN
9	BILLINGSLEY, William D., USN
10	MURRAY, James M., USN
11	MUSTIN, Henry C., USN
12	McILVAIN, William M., USMC
13	RICHARDSON, Holden C., USN
14	SAUFLEY, Richard C., USN
15	BRONSON, Clarence K., USN
16	WHITING, Kenneth, USN
17	MAXFIELD, Louis H., USN
18	McDONNELL, Edward O., USN
19	CAPEHART, Wadleigh, USN
20	SPENCER, Earl W. Jr., USN

The pioneers of Naval Aviation.

Marine Corps aviators trained alongside their Navy counterparts and shared the use of the aircraft listed above, although primarily the Marine Corps used the A-2, particularly after its conversion to the E-1.

The following narratives of each airplane's history provide an interesting commentary on how the Navy and Marines operated the airplanes. The detailed histories of the A-1 and A-2 are contained in their original logbooks that have been reproduced and are generally available for purchase or by loan from libraries (see the Bibliography). The histories of the remaining 12 airplanes are sketchy at best; most of the references were gleaned from books and from periodicals and newspapers of the early 20th century.

A-1 - The Navy's First Airplane

Ellyson and Towers conducted the initial testing of the A-1 at Annapolis, either alone or together. Their task was to learn how the airplane performed during the types of maneuvers that might be encountered in service with the fleet. They thoroughly tested the durability of the airframe and engine during the 40 flights that were performed at Annapolis between September 30 and December 20, 1911. The flights varied in duration from 3 minutes to 2 hours and 27 minutes.

The Curtiss engine and its accessories became problematic almost from the beginning of the flight tests at Annapolis. On October 11 Ellyson and Towers set out for a flight to Old Point Comfort but had to land the airplane 8 miles below Chesapeake Beach because of a broken safety wire and a missing bolt on the gas tank. Twenty minutes later they had to land to fix a broken carburetor bracket. Having fixed the bracket, they took off again, only to be forced down again because the #3, #4, #7, and #8 crankshaft bearings had burned out. They disassembled the airplane at Smith's Point and placed it on the USS *Bailey*, which had been summoned by wireless. The broken engine was shipped to Hammondsport and a replacement engine was received 10 days later.

The A-1 was quickly put back into flight test status, only to be damaged in a landing. The right lower wing and pontoon had to be replaced. The next day the water on the Bay was rough and the propeller struck a swell, breaking off a blade tip.

Having fixed all of the known problems, Ellyson and Towers planned the next flight as a two-hour endurance test of the weak parts of the airplane. They also planned to determine the human physical strains of a long flight. The practicality of the throw-over control column was also to be tested on the long flight. The destination of the endurance flight on October 25 was Ft. Monroe, VA, but two hours after taking off from Annapolis they landed at Milford Haven, VA because the engine was running hot due to a leaking radiator. The radiator was patched and the flight continued for another 25 minutes before they were forced to land again at Buckroe Beach, VA. The engine was running rough because the leaky radiator had sprayed water on the magneto. The magneto and radiator were fixed, and the next day they were able to complete the flight to Ft. Monroe.

The flight back to Annapolis was attempted on October 27, but the poor grade of gasoline that had been supplied by the Army prevented them from taking off. Another day was spent getting the proper grade of gasoline from Newport News. Several short segment flights were made over the next few days in an attempt to fly back to Annapolis. The water pump shaft sheared, the carburetor mounting broke, and the weather worsened with each passing day. The two intrepid aviators finally made it back to Annapolis on November 3. Towers said later, "We went down in a day and took a week to get back."

The radiator was repaired and the A-1 was back on flight test status a week later. On November 10 Ellyson and Towers conducted 10 short flights, some of which were familiarization flights for Navy personnel who rode as passengers. Ensign Herbster, Lieutenants Fitch and Castle, and Chiefs Duffy and Wiegand were each treated to flights of seven minutes in the newly repaired airplane.

On the afternoon of November 15 John Towers took the A-1 for a short flight when at an altitude of 150 ft. a gust of wind rolled the airplane into a 45-degree bank, resulting in a quick plunge into the cold waters below. Towers was thrown from the machine, the majority of which sank in 15 ft. deep water. Towers climbed onto the main pontoon, which remained afloat and waited 45 minutes for a boat to rescue him. Towers suffered minor cuts and bruises, a swollen face, and his left leg and ankle were badly sprained. There were no launches available to pull the wrecked aircraft from the water, so it remained submerged until the following day, when the weather worsened and prevented recovery. The A-1 was finally pulled out of the salt water on November 17, revealing a totally wrecked airplane. Wave action and the retrieval efforts had subsequently broken parts that had not been broken in the crash. The engine was overhauled, and the airframe was completely rebuilt using spare parts and newly ordered parts from Curtiss.

Both the new A-1 and John Towers were back in the air on December 19 and 20, once again providing familiarization flights for Navy personnel. One of the last flights of the year was made on December 20 when Towers and Ensign Charles Maddox attempted to flight test a wireless radio antenna. The experiment was a failure because the antenna wire broke every time it was reeled out from the airplane.

On December 29 the aviators were ordered to pack up their airplanes and equipment and ship it all to North Island, San Diego, where Glenn Curtiss had offered the use of his land for the Navy's winter Aviation Camp. The shipment left Annapolis on January 3, 1912 and arrived in San Diego on January 25. Several test flights were made with the A-1 after it had been assembled, each flight featuring problems with the radiator and water pump. The USS *Iris* provided support for the Navy fliers and their ground crews.

Ellyson and Towers spent the first two weeks of February making short familiarization flights for naval officers and enlisted men. Almost two dozen flights of this type were conducted. During these flights more problems were experienced with the engine and its accessories. The main pontoon started leaking and a replacement was taken from the spares pool. On one flight the propeller struck the water and had to be replaced. Finally, a main bearing bolt had worked loose and rattled through the

The Navy's first airplane, the Curtiss A-1 Hydroaeroplane, shown here in early 1912 on the beach at the Curtiss camp, North Island, San Diego. *Courtesy of the Glenn H. Curtiss Museum, Hammondsport, NY.*

The aftermath of Naval Constructor Holden Richardson's accident in the A-1, April 23, 1912, at San Diego. Richardson, shown standing on the prow of the main float, was not hurt and the A-1 was rebuilt. *U.S. Naval History and Heritage Command Photograph.*

crankcase, breaking five pistons, two cylinders and bending the camshaft and two connecting rods. Spare parts were ordered and the rebuilding of the engine began. The airplane did not fly again until late March. In the interim, Ellyson crashed the A-2, leaving the Navy without a serviceable airplane.

Curtiss loaned the Navy a dual control column to test in lieu of the throw-over column that had been used on the previous flights. Ellyson and Towers, both of whom found it satisfactory for dual instruction, tested it on two short flights. With the new dual control column installed on the A-1, flight instruction began on April 2. Naval Constructor Holden Richardson was the first student pilot; the instructor was John Towers. On his second solo flight, on April 23, Richardson inadvertently lifted the A-1 off the water while turning and buried the lower right wing in the water, causing the machine to turn upside down. The wreckage was towed to shore, disassembled and packed in crates for shipment to Annapolis, where the aviators had been ordered to return.

The flying camp at the Annapolis Experimental Station was reconstructed and was ready when the train carrying the wreckage of the A-1 and A-2 arrived on May 24. Within one week the A-1 was back on flying status, with Ellyson and Towers taking turns conducting short familiarization flights for a wide variety of individuals, including a U.S. Senator, J.A. Reed of Missouri. These flights continued until June 28 when engine trouble required a forced landing. The oil and water pumps failed, resulting in major damage to the bearings and camshaft. Once again, the engine was overhauled and flying resumed on July 13.

Preparations were made to test the A-1 on a compressed air catapult system that had been devised by Chambers and Richardson. Chambers wanted to demonstrate to the Navy that an airplane could be launched from a ship without the ship having to slow down. He also wanted to demonstrate that the launch system could be made very compact so that it did not interfere with the ship's warfighting capability. Chambers' catapult was a relatively short one, consisting of a tank for the compressed air, a piston and a series of cables that drove a wooden cart along a pair of rails. The airplane was simply placed on the cart with no hold-down device to secure the main

float. The catapult system was placed on the Santee dock at Annapolis, air lines were routed to the dock, and the catapult was tested by launching heavy timbers into the Severn River.

Initial catapult trials were conducted at Annapolis using the A-1. The entire setup is shown here on the Santee dock prior to the failed launch attempt. *U.S. Naval History and Heritage Command Photograph.*

On July 31, 1912 the A-1 was mounted on the cart, Ellyson took his seat on the airplane and prepared for launch. He pressed the throttle wide open and gave the "ready" signal. The initial acceleration along the track was so sudden that Ellyson was slammed back in his seat and his hands were yanked from the control wheel. About halfway down the track the airplane pitched up, stalled, and rolled to the left into the river. It all happened so quickly that Ellyson did not have time to react to the aircraft's violent pitch and roll. The airplane hit the water nose-first with the engine at maximum power. Ellyson was unhurt in the crash and immediately surfaced to begin directing the recovery of the A-1. But once again the A-1 had to be rebuilt after a plunge into salt water.

Chambers and Richardson went back to the drawing board and modified the catapult so that the initial release of the air piston was done more gradually, and a hold-down device was added to prevent the airplane from pitching up as it gained speed. The inventors would have to wait for an available airplane before they could repeat the experiment.

The A-1 logbook, which had been meticulously updated after every flight up to that point, simply stated "Launched from dock, machine wrecked." The logbook was signed "TG Ellyson, by JHT."

The A-1 was rebuilt once again and instructional flying commenced again on September 26 and continued into October. Chambers' newly modified catapult had been installed on a barge docked at the Washington Naval Yard, and Ellyson was ordered to fly the A-1 to Washington to continue the catapult testing. On October 26, Ellyson and Lt. Bernard L. Smith, USMC, prepared the A-1 for an early morning departure from Annapolis, intending to make a nonstop flight to the Navy Yard on the Potomac River. Pointing the A-1 into the wind and toward the beach, Ellyson eked a shallow climb from the Hydro, but it was not rising quickly enough to clear the trees. He banked the airplane to clear the trees but the machine lost altitude, impacted the river in a skid, and flipped over. Ellyson and Smith emerged from the wreckage unhurt but cold and wet.

The A-1 was hauled from the river once again, the last logbook entry stating simply: "Machine wrecked last flight. Expended, except motor. Not rebuilt."

A-2 – The Transformer

The A-2 was delivered to Annapolis as a landplane but it was not used very often because the landing field at Greenbury Point was too short for any meaningful work to be accomplished. In addition, Ellyson and Towers had a full workload on the A-1, as detailed in the previous section. The A-2 was shipped to San Diego along with the A-1 in early 1912 but it was not flown there until March. During one of the first flights at North Island, Ellyson was making a low pass over the Curtiss airfield when gusty air caused him to lose control and crash. The A-2 impacted the field nose-first and turned over, throwing Ellyson from the machine. He landed on his head, sustaining a strained neck and back, a sprained left ankle and serious lacerations and bruises. The A-2 was a total wreck, with the majority of the parts either damaged or broken. In their spare time the Navy crew at North Island began rebuilding the airplane as a hydroaeroplane, and it was used as a hydroaeroplane for the remainder of its life.

Ellyson and Towers used the A-2 at Annapolis mainly for training new aviators, and the airplane performed reasonably well, with the exception that the engine and its accessories failed frequently. The airplanes had been in service for almost a year, so the Navy mechanics had probably become very skilled at fixing the troublesome Curtiss engines. Towers felt comfortable enough with the machine to undertake an endurance test in the A-2. The airplane was fitted with additional fuel tanks and a supplemental water tank for the radiator. The wing tip extensions were added to the upper wing and on October 6, 1912 Towers took off at 6:49 AM and remained aloft for 6 hours, 10 minutes and 35 seconds, establishing a world record for hydroaeroplanes and setting a US record for any type of airplane.

Shown here at the Navy's first aviation base at Greenbury Point, MD, the Curtiss A-2 was initially used as a land-based trainer airplane but was later converted to a hydroaeroplane. *U.S. Naval History and Heritage Command Photograph.*

A few new pilots were quickly qualifying and had soloed in the months since the aviators returned from the winter camp at North Island. One of the new pilots, Lt. Laurance N. McNair, soloed on September 21 but made a poor water landing on October 27, flipping the A-2 on its back and breaking the pontoon, several wing parts and an aileron, but McNair emerged unhurt. On successive days the Navy had splashed their only two Hydros, The A-1 was written off, but the A-2 was rebuilt using the A-1's engine while its own engine was shipped back to Hammondsport for overhaul.

Intensive flight training began once again with Marine Lt. Bernard L. Smith soloing on December 2. He was the second Marine officer to solo, Lt. Alfred A. Cunningham having soloed in a Wright B-1 in May. Smith flew the A-2 for several weeks before the Annapolis camp was abandoned for a new winter camp at Guantanamo Bay. On January 15, 1913 Smith began a series of familiarization flights from the Guantanamo base. Throughout January and February Smith was able to make almost daily flights, interrupted only by continuing engine problems. The rebuilt A-2 engine was finally replaced with the A-1 engine, which provided some degree of consistent performance.

Returning to Annapolis in April, Smith continued as the primary A-2 pilot, with Towers flying the machine on occasion. But now the A-1 engine woes resumed and continued through the summer. The last flight as an A-2 was accomplished on June 11, 1913.

The Navy had decided to convert the A-2 into an amphibian, consequently the airplane was disassembled and shipped to Hammondsport for the transformation by the Curtiss factory. Captain Chambers was the originator of the amphibian concept, arguing that the Navy and Marines needed an airplane that could operate on the water and on shore. He felt that ship-to-shore communication between Navy and Marine units would be much faster using an amphibian. The idea was tried out on the original A-1, using the *Triad* landing gear, but the flimsy wheels were not sturdy enough for takeoff and landing on land, and the added drag of the wheels in the water and in the air seriously degraded the performance of the A-1.

Navy aviation personnel at the 1913 winter camp, Guantanamo Bay. Officers shown are: Lt. (jg) P.N.L. Bellinger, 1st Lt. B.L. Smith (USMC), 1st Lt. A.A. Cunningham (USMC), Lt. J.H. Towers, Ens. V.D. Herbster, Ens. W.D. Billingsley, and Ens. G. deC. Chevalier. Note the goat and dog mascots. *U.S. Naval History and Heritage Command Photograph.*

Not easily deterred by the *Triad's* failure, Chambers assigned Naval Constructor Holden C. Richardson to design a new amphibian machine, named the OWL (Over Water and Land). The OWL's official Navy designation was E-1. The E-1 incorporated several lessons learned from the *Triad* experience, including landing gear wheels that retracted into the main float, on which the pilots sat, enclosed by a large cockpit fairing. The wings, tail and engine installations were virtually unchanged from the A-2. Richardson's final design was a compromise between an optimized flying boat hull and a design that simply added an enclosed cockpit on top of a short pontoon. The forced marriage of cockpit and pontoon was not a happy one as the Navy was to discover during the initial testing phase of the OWL.

Lt. Bernard L. Smith was the natural choice for project pilot on the OWL, given his experience on the A-2 and his USMC experience. Water trials began on Lake Keuka on September 23, 1913 and after some initial problems with aerodynamic lateral stability issues and water-borne longitudinal problems, Smith made the first flight on the following day. Richardson flew as a passenger on the third flight, but Smith noted that the airplane was nose-heavy, difficult to land without adding power, and he was unable to lift off from the water. Smith was worried about the safety of using the machine for "land work" so the wheels were removed and covers placed over the wheel wells. Chambers must have been upset about Smith's decision to stop the land-based flying because he immediately ordered Smith to continue with the flights from the runway at Hammondsport.

Smith resumed his wheeled flights with the E-1 on September 30, but with no effective braking the airplane had to be muscled to a stop by the ground crew. The bottom of the float dragged on the ground when it was landed on all three wheels, so Smith had to land on the aft two wheels, further lengthening the stopping distance. Rates of climb were very low, especially with a passenger aboard. During a flight to perfect his landing technique on October 6, Smith bounced the E-1 four times before taking to the air and landing on Lake Keuka. He wrote in the E-1's logbook that he "did not consider it safe to land with a passenger." A few flights were made during October and November during which engine problems cropped up again, but it was obvious that the OWL in its present form was not suitable for operation on land or on water. On November 25 the airplane was partially disassembled and sent to the factory to be rebuilt.

Opposite
Top: On the beach at Hammondsport, NY, the A-2 is shown after its transformation into the E-1 OWL (Over Water and Land) in late 1913. Flight test pilots are left to right, Naval Constructor Holden Richardson and Lt. Bernard L. Smith, USMC. *Courtesy of the Glenn H. Curtiss Museum, Hammondsport, NY.*

Bottom: Curtiss factory personnel are shown taking one last opportunity to tune up the E-1 OWL before its first trials on Lake Keuka, NY, September 23, 1913. *Courtesy of the Glenn H. Curtiss Museum, Hammondsport, NY.*

Above: First water trials of the E-1 OWL on Lake Keuka, NY, piloted by Lt. Bernard L. Smith, USMC. The OWL was an experimental amphibious hydroaeroplane intended for use by the U.S. Marine Corps. *Courtesy of the Museum of Flight, Seattle, WA.*

The OWL emerged from the factory in January 1914 with a redesigned shock absorbing landing gear and a more aerodynamically shaped cockpit enclosure. USMC Lt. William M. McIlvain assisted Lt. Smith with the evaluation flights at Hammondsport. They found the airplane "left the water with ease" but the control on the water was so poor that they could not turn the E-1 to avoid the shore as they taxied in. The wing was damaged and the landing gear had to be overhauled. In spite of the poor performance of the new OWL (sometimes referred to as the OWL II), orders were given to ship the airplane to Pensacola, Florida, the new home of the Naval Aeronautic Station. The E-1 and crew embarked on the USS *Hancock* on February 2, 1914 and flying started again on March 4. Apparently runway work was accomplished during the early flights because on March 25 the logbook states that a plank on the bottom of the float was ripped off, "probably done on runway."

The logbook ends somewhat mysteriously on April 1, 1914, simply noting "taking boat off planes." One report states that the E-1 was shipped as spare parts in support of the Vera Cruz action in April 1914, but the logbook is mute on the use of the airplane until a few entries appear in late 1915. The airplane had been redesignated AX-1 in March 1914 and was being used for material tests. Lt. Clarence K. Bronson was the pilot of the last flight of the AX-1 on November 27 at Pensacola; it was a material test during which both wings were broken. The airplane had performed 575 flights as the A-2, more than 90 as the E-1, and an unknown number as the AX-1. The Navy did not purchase another amphibian type until well after World War I.

The A-3 – Workhorse and War-horse
The Navy's third Curtiss airplane, the A-3 was delivered in October 1912, the month that the A-1 was written off in a crash at Annapolis. The A-1 was being flown to Washington, DC to conduct a second round of catapult trials when it crashed. The A-2 was unavailable at the time because it was being repaired after an accident at Annapolis. The Navy decided to press on with the catapult testing using the A-3, consequently Ellyson began flying the brand-new A-3 that had been delivered to the Washington Navy Yard. He made several test hops before pronouncing the airplane ready for the catapult trials.

At the Navy Yard the barge on which Captain Chambers' catapult had been placed was not as high off the water as the setup at Annapolis had been, thereby providing a slightly safer launch facility. Several test launches were made with dummy loads simulating the weight of the A-3, meanwhile Ellyson readied the A-3 for the test.

On November 12, 1912, the A-3 was secured to the car by the new hold-down device. Ellyson secured himself in the left-hand seat, firmly grabbed the control column and waited for the initial kick from the catapult. The airplane received a

good jolt from the catapult, but Ellyson held on and the airplane was quickly free of the catapult's car, which had dropped into the Potomac as the A-3 climbed away from the Navy Yard in an easy spiral. Chambers and Richardson were elated with the success of their invention, Ellyson was undoubtedly happy not to have gotten another dunking, and Glenn Curtiss called it "the greatest aviation advance since wheels replaced skids for aeroplane landing gear." A month later Ellyson repeated the test using the Navy's first flying boat, the Curtiss C-1.

Ellyson's two catapult launches were the beginning of a long series of development tests, intended not only to improve the system, but to determine the best ways to incorporate the device on a Navy ship. The "cats" were modified, enlarged, and ultimately perfected on cruisers and battleships in World War II. And a highly modified version of Chambers' catapult system is in use on today's aircraft carriers.

The A-3 was shipped to Guantanamo Bay in January 1913 to participate in tests designed to determine the role of the airplane in the fleet. Together with the A-2 the two airplanes also provided basic flight training for new pilots. The new Curtiss flying boats were taking over much of the advanced flying, but the hydros were considered better suited for training. It was becoming obvious that the Navy needed a year-round base for their embryonic fleet of airplanes. Moving the aircraft back and forth from Annapolis to Cuba or California was not an efficient way to use the Navy's meager aviation funding resources. Guantanamo was deemed too remote for efficiently supplying the aviators with their daily needs, and Annapolis was too cold in the winter. With an expanding fleet of airplanes, including the new Curtiss flying boats, the Navy decided that a permanent base was required.

An existing Navy base at Pensacola, Florida was chosen as the site for the Navy's first permanent base for its fledgling aeronautical unit based primarily on its warm year-round temperatures and calm winds. The base was located on Pensacola Bay, which was fairly large and provided relatively smooth water for initial water-based flight training. The open waters of the Gulf of Mexico were a short five-minute flight away, providing the open sea conditions required for advanced flight training and some experimental work. There was also ample land area available on the base to construct airfields for land-based flight training. And there was a

Opposite
Top: The A-3 is readied for the second set of Navy catapult tests, this time at the Washington Navy Yard, November 1912. *U.S. Naval History and Heritage Command Photograph.*

Bottom: The U.S. Navy's first successful launch of an airplane by catapult was made on November 12, 1912 at the Washington Navy Yard. Piloted by Lt. T.G. Ellyson, the Curtiss A-3 is depicted here ready for launch. The following month a Curtiss flying boat was launched from this catapult. *Courtesy of the Glenn H. Curtiss Museum, Hammondsport, NY.*

Below: Complete with newly added wing tip extension panels, the A-3 is brought ashore by Navy bluejackets at Fisherman's Point, Guantanamo Bay during exercises with the fleet in early 1913. *Courtesy of the San Diego Air & Space Museum.*

Naval Aeronautic Station, Pensacola, Florida, March 1914, showing the southwestern waterfront, aircraft launching ramps, and tent hangars. The western wharf and Building 27-B are in the background. The airplanes shown are (from front to back), Curtiss flying boat, C-type; Curtiss Hydroaeroplane A-3; Curtiss flying boat, C-2; Curtiss flying boat, C-type; Wright hydroaeroplane B-3; Curtiss flying boat, C-type; Curtiss "OWL II" amphibian E-1; and Curtiss Hydroaeroplane A-4. The tails of A-3, C-2, and B-3 are marked "USN." E-1's tail is marked "USMC." *U.S. Naval History and Heritage Command Photograph NH 2275.*

substantial amount of beachfront property for the placement of hangars and slips for the Navy's seaplanes.

On January 20, 1914 the entire U.S. Navy aviation unit, consisting of nine officers, 23 men, 7 aircraft, and portable tent hangars, arrived at Pensacola on the USS *Mississippi* and *Orion*. Lt. John H. Towers was the officer in charge of the training unit, but the new Naval Aeronautic Station at Pensacola was placed under the command of LCDR. Henry C. Mustin, who also was in command of the station ship, the USS *Mississippi*.

After the E-1 arrived at Pensacola in February there were three Curtiss Hydroaeroplanes at Pensacola: the E-1, A-3 and the newly acquired A-4. The A-3 had been upgraded with wingtip extensions and an enlarged main float sometime in 1913. The rest of the aircraft consisted of four Curtiss flying boats and a Wright

Left: Wearing leather boots and puttees, Lt. John Towers and an unidentified pilot trainee are shown being carried by two sailors through the surf to their awaiting Curtiss Hydroaeroplane. *National Naval Aviation Museum, Pensacola, Photo 2008.104.001.022.*

Below: The aftermath of a fire on a Curtiss Hydroaeroplane at Pensacola, circa 1914-1915. The fire quickly destroyed the doped fabric covering, revealing the sparse skeletal outline of the Hydro's wooden structure. The Navy later required a hand-held fire extinguisher to be carried onboard. *National Naval Aviation Museum, Pensacola, Photo 2008.104.001.050.*

hydro, designated the B-3. Flight training began with a somber note: on January 16, Lt. (j.g.) James Murray crashed the Burgess D-1 on the water and drowned.

Accidents continued to occur, although without the loss of life. Several incidents involving on-board fires were reported, resulting in an order to attach a Pyrene fire extinguisher to each airplane. To reduce the number of accidents, the Navy developed an investigation and reporting system called a "trouble report" that aimed at alerting the chain of command to fix problem areas.

Ensigns Godfrey de C. Chevalier and Melvin L. Stolz survived the crash of the A-3 close to the Pensacola waterfront in March 1914. From a pier and from the USS *Mississippi*, scores of Navy men watch the recovery of the mostly submerged hydro. The intact airplane was hoisted onto shore, but it was completely soaked in salt water. *National Naval Aviation Museum, Pensacola, Photo 2008.104.001.013.*

The U.S. Navy's first combat air group embarked aboard the USS *Mississippi* en route to Vera Cruz, Mexico, in April 1914. The A-3 is on top of the rear gun turret and the Curtiss C-3 flying boat is on the aft main deck, its tail section hanging over the side of the ship. Note boom rigged for hoisting aircraft. *National Archives Photo 80-G-461428.*

Opposite
Top: Lts. Bellinger and Saufley stand on the A-3 as it is lowered to the water from the USS *Mississippi*. Scouting missions were flown at Vera Cruz in support of the Marines on shore. Note the thirteen-star "boat" flags on the A-3's wingtip struts. *National Archives Photo 80-G-391981.*

Bottom: The AH-3 on the water, awaiting a hoist aboard ship. *U.S. Naval History and Heritage Command Photograph 459635.*

Less than a month after Murray's crash, Ensigns Godfrey de C. Chevalier and Melvin L. Stolz were flying the A-3 along the Pensacola waterfront when a gust of wind flipped them into the water. The airplane was completely submerged except for the main pontoon, onto which Chevalier and Stolz had scrambled. The two water-soaked airmen were able to direct the recovery of the A-3 from the pontoon while scores of Navy men watched the recovery operation from a pier and from the USS *Mississippi*. The mostly intact airplane was hoisted onto shore, but it was completely soaked in salt water.

Apparently the A-3 was not too badly damaged because it was ready for deployment on April 19 when the Navy ordered the Pensacola aeronautic unit to depart for Mexican waters in support of a US intervention. Towers, Smith and Chevalier were assigned to leave for Tampico on the USS *Birmingham* with two Curtiss flying boats and two bamboo tail hydroaeroplanes, the A-4 and the AX-1 (OWL II). A second Navy Department communication arrived soon after, ordering Mustin to assemble a second set of airplanes on the USS *Michigan* and to sail with 500 Marines to Vera Cruz. The A-3 and the C-3 flying boat were loaded onto the old battleship, the A-3 on top of the rear gun turret and the C-3 on the aft main deck, its tail section hanging over the side of the ship.

The two ships arrived at their stations on April 24, with the *Mississippi* anchored outside the breakwater at Vera Cruz. Flying at Vera Cruz began almost immediately, the C-3 searching for mines and looking for the Mexican ground forces outside the city. It has been noted that this was the first action by a warplane in support of a combat operation. Most of the flying was done in support of the ground forces that were trying to locate the Mexican forces, and to this end the airplanes proved their worth in being able to gather a large amount of reconnaissance information in a short amount of time.

The main fighting at Vera Cruz had taken place in the first three days of the operation, during which time the airplanes were en route to Mexico, so the city was peaceful enough for the airplanes to be moved from the USS *Mississippi* to the beach inside the breakwater. The water was smoother inside the breakwater, and the airplanes could be launched more rapidly than from the *Mississippi's* deck. Flying the A-3 on a scouting mission on May 6, Lieutenants P.N.L. Bellinger and Richard C. Saufley were unable to locate Mexican troops, but when they returned to base, they found a bullet hole in the airplane's canvas covering. Thus damaged, the A-3 became the first Navy airplane to be struck by hostile fire.

The airplanes flew daily support missions throughout May but the heat, humidity and salt water were taking a toll on the Navy's men and their airplanes.

The airplanes were only able to fly short 15-minute missions by the end of May. The military intervention was now a land-based operation, with the Army taking over the scouting missions in land-based airplanes. Mustin received orders to return to Pensacola, sailing on June 12.

The Vera Cruz operation had proved the value of the Navy's airplanes in support of the fleet. The official order to return to Pensacola included praise that the actions of the Aeronautic Service were in keeping with the great accomplishments of the Navy during the Mexican intervention. The A-3 (by then known as the AH-3) had proved its value to the Navy fleet at sea and to the Marines ashore. The in-service experience was invaluable in helping to set standards for future water-based Navy airplanes.

The A-4 – From the Spare Parts Bin to Flight

In early 1914 the only Hydro available for training was the A-3, and because the flying boats were considered unsuitable for the purpose, an order was given to construct the A-4 from spare parts at Pensacola.

On March 27, 1914, per General Order 88, the original designations for Navy aircraft were changed to two letters and a number, of which the first letter designated the class, the second within a class, and the number the order in which the aircraft in a class were acquired.

Four classes were defined:

Opposite
Top: Planes and personnel at the U.S. Navy's beach camp at Vera Cruz, Mexico, April 1914. Lt. Patrick N.L. Bellinger is shown at the far right. The airplanes are the Curtiss C-3 flying boat and the Curtiss A-3 Hydroaeroplane. *National Naval Aviation Museum, Pensacola, Photo 2008.104.001.215.*

Bottom: Lt. Patrick N.L. Bellinger, Naval Aviator Number 8, pictured here on a Curtiss Hydroaeroplane at the Naval Aeronautic Station Pensacola, Florida. While on a reconnaissance mission over Vera Cruz on May 6, 1914, Lt. Bellinger's hydroaeroplane, the Curtiss AH-3, was hit by rifle fire, thus incurring the first marks of combat on a U.S. Navy aircraft. *National Naval Aviation Museum, Pensacola, Photo 2008.104.001.068.*

Top: Personnel prepare aircraft for observation flights that were part of U.S. Navy operations in the aftermath of the Vera Cruz insurrection, 1914. The airplanes deteriorated in the hot sun and salt-water environment, requiring frequent maintenance to the airframe and engines. *National Naval Aviation Museum, Pensacola, Photo 2008.104.001.216.*

Above: Aviation encampment on the beach near Vera Cruz, Mexico in 1914, showing the rudimentary facilities in which Navy personnel lived and worked to support a handful of flying boats and hydroaeroplanes. *National Naval Aviation Museum, Pensacola, Photo 2008.104.001.272.*

A – all heavier than air craft
D – airships or dirigibles
B – balloons
K – kites

Within the A class, L, H , B, X and C stood for land machines, hydroaeroplanes, flying boats, combination land and water machines, and convertibles, respectively.

Thus, the A-3 became the AH-3, the A-2 (E-1) became the AX-1. In a departure from the new designation codes, the A-4 became the AH-2. The AH-2 appeared on the list of active airplanes in July 1915, but the final disposition of the airplane is unknown.

The AH-8 – First in Its Class

The first two airplanes purchased by the Navy in the new numbering system were the Curtiss AH-8 and AH-9. Both of the new airplanes and indeed, all of the subsequent Curtiss Hydroaeroplanes were referred to as AH-8 type. This has caused some confusion in the identification of individual aircraft of the AH-8 type. The authors have been careful to identify individual aircraft by their respective AH- numbers only when they have been so identified in written material. Many times an "AH-8 type" is the only identification available.

Curtiss incorporated many changes in the AH-8 that improved the operability of the Hydro. The engines were upgraded with higher horsepower Model OX units, the central float was enlarged, and wingtip extension panels were added to the upper wing. In December 1915 Lt. Richard C. Saufley used the AH-8 to fly a 60-mile mission over the Gulf of Mexico in support of Navy scouting experiments.

The upgraded AH-8 Curtiss Hydroaeroplane furnished Naval Aviators with additional engine power, enlarged main floats and other refinements. Shown here at Hammondsport, NY in 1914, a civilian version of the AH-8 awaits delivery to its customer. The U.S. Navy ordered five Hydros of this type. *Courtesy of the Museum of Flight, Seattle, WA.*

The AH-9 – The Widow Maker

Two of the more tragic airplane crashes at Pensacola involved the AH-9, which was acquired by the Navy in 1914. An AH-8 type, it appears to have been a sister ship to the original AH-8.

On May 8, 1915, Lt. (j.g.) Melvin L. Stolz took the AH-9 out for a flight to familiarize himself with the hydroaeroplane. Stolz had not flown for over nine months and had asked for permission for a flight to qualify as a naval aviator. Under the guidance of Lt. Richard Saufley, Stolz was given permission to fly the AH-9, the last flight he would make. Witnesses saw Stolz take off from the beach and make a slow climb, followed by a turn toward the bay, when the Hydro suddenly pitched down and impacted the water.

Underwater rescue efforts failed to immediately free Stolz from his seat, but when he was finally brought to the surface it was discovered that the engine had crushed his head. The cause of the accident was attributed to a stall in a turn, caused by an inexperienced pilot. The Hydros were very difficult to fly; they had a very narrow operating speed envelope, and the sharp leading edge of the wing's airfoil caused a very precipitous stall. The stall came on so quickly and so precipitously that pilots had very little time to react. The pilots did not have airspeed indicators to rely on to keep them away from stalling speed, and the engines were not powerful enough to accelerate quickly away from stalling speed.

Arguments among Navy brass about the safety of pusher airplanes continued even after the Stolz accident. Some argued that Stolz was merely inexperienced, while some argued that tractor-type airplanes were inherently safer because the engines were in front of the flight crew. Meanwhile, more Hydros were ordered from Curtiss and the training at Pensacola continued.

The AH-9 was rebuilt over the next year at Pensacola under the direction of Lt. Saufley. New F-boat type wings were obtained from Curtiss, making the AH-9 look more like the newest Hydros that were then being delivered in 1916. Sadly, Saufley was killed in the rebuilt AH-9 on June 9, 1916. He was concluding an endurance flight of eight hours when observers saw his plane nose over and crash onto Santa Rosa Island, off Pensacola. Saufley was killed instantly, his head, chest and legs crushed by the engine. A board of inquiry placed the blame on an inexperienced mechanic who had failed to properly attach the elevator hinges. The elevators had come off the Hydro in flight, causing the crash.

Lt. (j.g.) Melvin L. Stolz died in the crash of the AH-9 hydroaeroplane on May 8, 1915, the first in a series of crashes that led to the effective grounding of the Navy's Curtiss pusher hydroaeroplanes in 1916. Shown here is Ensign Stolz, when he first reported for aviation duty in October 1913. *National Naval Aviation Museum, Pensacola, Photo 2008.104.001.036.*

Left: Lt. Richard C. Saufley was one of the more proficient Naval aviators, setting several altitude and endurance records in Navy aircraft. His death in the crash of the rebuilt AH-9 on June 9, 1916 caused the Navy to withdraw the Curtiss Hydros from its fleet of training aircraft. *National Naval Aviation Museum, Pensacola, Photo 2008.104.001.059.*

Below: Heralding the end of the bamboo-tailed Curtiss Hydroaeroplane era in early 1916, a newly acquired Martin S tractor floatplane is shown here with Lt. Richard C. Saufley. Saufley was the last Naval Aviator to die in the crash of a Curtiss Hydroaeroplane before they were relegated to the role of flight testing pontoons. *George Grantham Bain Collection, Prints & Photographs Division, Library of Congress, LC-DIG-ggbain-21510.*

Contemporary U.S. Navy Hydroaeroplanes

In addition to the Curtiss airplanes, the U.S. Navy operated several other hydroaeroplanes manufactured by the Wright and Burgess companies.

The U.S. Navy operated three Wright Model C-H airplanes during the period from 1912 to 1914. They were designated B-1 through B-3 by the Navy. Navy personnel at Annapolis built the B-2 from spare parts after the B-1 crashed. The performance of the airplanes was marginal and after a crash that killed Ensign W.D. Billingsley, no additional airplanes of the type were ordered. The airplanes were assigned designation numbers AH-4, AH-5, and AH-6.

The Navy also acquired two swept-wing tail-less Burgess-Dunne hydroaeroplanes, designated AH-7 and AH-10. The AH-7 had open, side-by-side seating with a 90-hp Curtiss engine. Its sister airplane, the AH-10, had semi-enclosed seating for the flight crew, and was also powered by a 90-hp Curtiss engine.

Flying the AH-10, Lt. Patrick Bellinger established a new American altitude record for seaplanes by flying to 10,000 feet on April 23, 1915. The airplanes were used for aerial gunnery and bombing experiments.

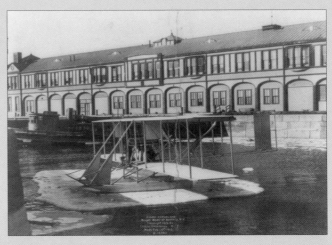

The U.S. Navy operated 3 Wright hydroaeroplanes, similar in configuration to the civilian model shown here at the Battery, NYC, in February 1912. All three Navy airplanes were out of service before 1915. *Prints & Photographs Division, Library of Congress, LC-USZ62-88940.*

Above: One of two tailless Burgess-Dunne hydroaeroplanes operated briefly by the Navy, the AH-7 was used for aerial gunnery experiments. *National Naval Aviation Museum, Pensacola, Photo 2008.104.001.109.*

Below: Sister ship to the AH-7, the Burgess-Dunne AH-10 hydroaeroplane was used for experimental bombing tests. *National Naval Aviation Museum, Pensacola, Photo 2008.104.001.112.*

The AH-12 – Boats Afloat!

Delivered to the Navy in 1915 together with the AH-11, the AH-12 was a standard two-seat trainer that was also used as a test bed for a twin-float design. Naval Constructor Holden Richardson designed and tested the floats in 1915, with good results.

It had been predicted that the floats would steer poorly when they were planing, but they proved to be very stable. Even when one float was forced to make contact ahead of the other in landing, no slewing was encountered. Although the twin floats were shorter than the standard single float, their longitudinal stability was satisfactory, even in moderate sea states when water was taken over the submerged bows.

Left: Testing an experimental twin-float design at Pensacola, circa 1916. The pilot is Lt. P.N.L. Bellinger and the airplane is a modified Curtiss AH-13 Hydroaeroplane. *U.S. Naval History and Heritage Command Photograph NH 74076.*

Below: The Curtiss AH-13 Hydroaeroplane equipped with experimental twin V-bottom floats designed by Naval Constructor Holden Richardson. Testing at Pensacola was successful and paved the way for application to future seaplane designs. *U.S. Naval History and Heritage Command Photograph.*

A triple-float design was tested in early 1916 with mixed results. The lateral stability was improved over the single-float plus tip-float design, but the side floats developed suction on their inboard stern surfaces that caused severe ground looping. Nevertheless, scaled up versions of the triple floats were applied to the A-82, the first U.S. government airplane built at the Washington Navy Yard.

Above: Based on successful scale model testing in 1915, experimental triple floats were attached to the AH-12 and tested in early 1916. The objective was to provide lateral stability in the water without the use of wingtip floats. *National Naval Aviation Museum, Pensacola, Photo 2008.104.001.114.*

Right: The experimental triple floats created fairly large wakes compared with the single centerline float. Several float designs were tried before satisfactory performance was achieved. *U.S. Naval History and Heritage Command Photograph NH74078.*

Wreckage of the AH-12 equipped with experimental triple floats, March 29, 1916. Instability caused by the outboard floats' hydrodynamic design caused severe ground looping. The floats' designs were altered and the instability was removed. *National Naval Aviation Museum, Pensacola, Photo 2008.104.001.232.*

The AH-13, AH-14, and AH-15 – Record Setters

Acquired in late 1915, this trio of training aircraft was also used by Lt. Richard C. Saufley to set several altitude records. The machines were equipped with a Curtiss engine developing 90 horsepower and a Paragon three-bladed propeller. The airplanes were the last Hydros to be delivered with the Model E wings.

Taking off from Pensacola on March 9, 1916, Lt. Saufley flew the AH-13 to an altitude of 12,400 ft., achieving that altitude in 74 minutes with a light load. Saufley had previously flown the AH-14 to an altitude of 11,975 ft. on December 3, 1915, and prior to that he coaxed the AH-15 up to 11,056 ft. on November 30, 1915.

The AH-14 was destroyed in a crash at Pensacola on May 24, 1916. Lt. James V. Rockwell had taken the Hydro out for a high altitude test, but about an hour into the flight he was seen spiraling down and finally crashing into the water. Lt. Rockwell was found strapped to his seat, his head crushed by the engine. The cause of the crash was determined to be either a stall or failure of the bamboo tail outrigger.

The Navy's debate over the safety of the Hydro's pusher configuration continued. The official report pointed out the dangers inherent in the Hydro's design, but the

The AH-13 was delivered to the Navy in late 1915. Note the three-bladed propeller and the pilot's padded backrest. "Skid fins" have been moved outboard to the center wing posts. *U.S. Naval History and Heritage Command Photograph.*

top Navy brass effectively rejected the report. They argued that adding proper instruments would allow the pilots to fly the Hydros without having to rely on seat-of-the-pants control of the aircraft.

The AH-16, AH-17, AH-18 – Last of the Breed

Delivered to the Navy in early 1916, the AH-16, AH-17, and AH-18 were the last Curtiss Hydroaeroplanes operated by the U.S. Navy. Based on the number of changes compared to the earlier models, the trio could have been given a separate type classification. But in some written material they were still referred to as AH-8 types.

Naval Aviator class, Pensacola, 1916. Officers are left to right, Forde, Monfort, Mitscher, instructors McDonnell and Johnson, Strickland, Gillespie, Young, and Dichman. *U.S. Naval History and Heritage Command Photograph.*

Opposite
Top: The final three U.S. Navy aircraft in the Curtiss Hydro-aeroplane series were delivered in early 1916. Each of the airplanes, AH-16, -17, and -18, was equipped with newly designed wings, the same wings as the new Curtiss Model F flying boats. *U.S. Naval History and Heritage Command Photograph NH74074.*

Middle: An F-winged Hydro on the launching ramp at Pensacola, 1916. The upper wing's airfoil shape is shown to good advantage. The airplane in the background is one of the Navy's Burgess-Dunne hydroaeroplanes. *National Naval Aviation Museum, Pensacola, Photo 2008.104.001.209.*

Bottom: The AH-18 was the final Curtiss Hydroaeroplane delivered to the U.S. Navy. Seen here at Pensacola being maneuvered by bluejackets, the airplane had a very short career as a training vehicle for Naval Aviators. *Courtesy of the Glenn H. Curtiss Museum, Hammondsport, NY.*

The distinguishing features of the airplanes were the incorporation of F-boat wings, larger wing tip floats, more powerful engines, and an enlarged main float. The new main floats were designed with a deeper stern to prevent the Hydro from tipping over backwards when adrift. The wings were of simpler construction. The upper wing, for example, was made up of two parts instead of the seven parts on the previous types.

All three Hydros were sent to Guantanamo Bay on the USS *North Carolina*, departing Pensacola on March 20, 1916. Their task was to participate with the fleet in spotting the shell splashes during firing exercises, but lacking radios with which to communicate with the fleet, the exercises were basically without meaning. And of course the usual engine problems plagued the Hydros, limiting the amount of time they could be employed as spotters for the fleet.

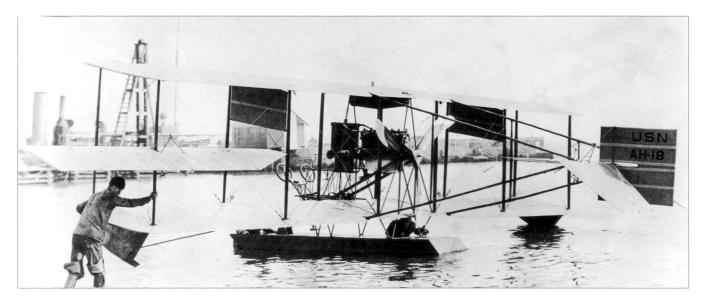

Below: The AH-12 was painted in an experimental checkerboard camouflage pattern to test its effectiveness. The pattern consisted of 6-inch squares except on the ailerons where they measured 4 inches. Colors are unknown but shades of gray are a possibility. *U.S. Naval History and Heritage Command Photograph.*

Bottom left: The F-winged Hydro shown here has been painted with the World War I insignia that became effective on May 20, 1917 by order of the Secretary of the Navy, Josephus Daniels. Unfortunately the wording of the order was ambiguous about the correct orientation of the "star in circle" insignia, consequently this airplane's star was applied upside down! *U.S. Naval History and Heritage Command Photograph.*

Bottom right: Clipped wings! This "skimmer" was used to train new pilots in water-taxi techniques. Taken in June 1916, this photo can be viewed as an ironic symbol of the Navy's order to ground the Hydros in the summer of 1916. The "skimmer" pilot is Lt. Earl W. Spencer, Jr., who later married and divorced Bessie Wallis Warfield, the future Duchess of Windsor. *U.S. Naval History and Heritage Command Photograph NH74079.*

The End of the Line

After the crashes of Stolz, Rockwell, and Saufley the Navy Department finally reconsidered the recommendations from the three accident investigations. At the end of July 1916 the Chief of Naval Operations, Admiral W.S. Benson, grounded the Curtiss Hydroaeroplanes and ordered that new tractor-type aircraft be purchased for training Navy pilots.

As part of his grounding order, the CNO allowed the Hydros to remain in service as test vehicles for advanced float design, presumably flown only by experienced pilots. The remaining Hydros were used for other tests as well, notably as a camouflage paint test vehicle. At least one Hydro was in service in 1917 after the U.S. declared war on Germany because one official Navy photo shows the Hydro in flight with the new U.S. national insignia painted on its wing.

When the CNO gave his order to ground the Hydros, Curtiss was still in the process of delivering airplanes that had been ordered by the Navy. It is unknown how many airplanes were involved in the order; perhaps as many as six. At least one of the new airplanes was shipped to the Washington Navy Yard in 1916 and put into storage. Early in 1928 the crated Hydro, which had never been flown, was assembled by volunteers at Anacostia Naval Air Station and put into flying condition. Commander Holden Richardson made a few flights over the Potomac River in March 1928 to demonstrate the progress that had been achieved in aviation in the 25 years since the Wright brothers' first flight at Kitty Hawk. While Richardson's flights were not official Navy missions, they do represent the last time that the U.S. Navy flew an original Curtiss Hydroaeroplane.

Russia

In 1909 the idea of providing the Russian Imperial Fleet with airplanes was already in the air, with both supporters and detractors among naval officers of all ranks. From time to time the Navy Ministry chancellery received reports and papers describing the evident benefits that airplanes could bring to the fleet but, probably, the first actual step towards the establishment of naval aviation was made in January 1910*, when the Air Fleet Department was established within the Fleet Strengthening Committee by proposal of Captain L. Matsievich. The purpose of the new structure was the development of aviation in Russia. The department was allotted considerable funds for the standards of the time to train pilots and mechanics and to purchase airplanes. After some time the plans of the Department included the organization of flight schools at Gatchina and also at Sevastopol, the main base of the Russian Black Sea Fleet. (*Note: All dates in the Russian part of this chapter are from the Julian calendar, which was used in Russia during that time period.)

The Officer Pilot School at Sevastopol was founded in November. Two months earlier, in September 1910, near Sevastopol, the Aeronautical Station Commander Lieutenant Dorozhinsky flew the first airplane, an Antoinette, in the purchase of which he participated personally. In autumn 1909 Dorozhinsky was sent to France to buy an airplane. Eventually, he reached an agreement with the Antoinette Company. While the airplane was under construction, he attended flight courses that were included in the price of the contract, and was the first Russian officer who received a pilot's licence.

In spring 1911 the school already had several land-based airplanes of various types, purchased in France by the Air Fleet Department. In addition to Antoinette, Farmans and Blériots were used. This allowed Russian aviators not only to train intensively, but also to research the possibilities for practical use of airplanes in the interest of the fleet. In April an experiment was carried out during which some airplanes of the Officer Pilot School escorted a squadron of Russian ships. To simulate bombing, oranges were dropped on the ironclad, and one of the oranges actually hit the vessel. In May, in the waters off Sevastopol, an experiment was made to search for a submarine from an airplane. At the appointed place, a submarine running underwater was identified by the breaking wave of its periscope and photographed.

However, flying over the sea in land-based airplanes, which then were not particularly reliable, was too dangerous. For aerial reconnaissance and surveillance the navy needed airplanes able to take off and land on water. Information that seaplanes were already being built and flying in Europe and in America reached Sevastopol. In the summer of 1911, by proposal of Lieutenant Dorozhinsky, it was decided to mount floats on one of the two Antoinettes given to the fleet by the Officer Pilot School. The floats were made at the local woodworking plant. The first float model was unsuccessful, but the second set gave the airplane decent stability on water, and in June the pilots tried to fly it. The airplane could not gain the speed required for takeoff. As the engine speed increased, the floats submerged, and the propeller kicked up water spray and did not give the necessary traction. The power of the 50-hp engine was definitely not sufficient to fly the rather heavy Antoinette off the water.

The failure with the float-equipped Antoinette and the acute need for seaplanes forced the fleet to consider the purchase of aircraft outside of Russia. As early as July the Navy Ministry received a report from the Head of the Sevastopol Port with the proposal to send a group of navy officers to Europe, to study the current achievements of foreign companies and to purchase the most successful seaplanes for the navy. The officers chosen for the task were the Head of the Communication Service of the Black Sea Fleet, 2nd Rank Captain Kedrin, and Lieutenant Dorozhinsky. By that time Kedrin already knew about the work of Glenn Curtiss. A marine agent in Washington, Vasiliev, in March 1911 had sent the general staff a detailed description of an airplane made by an American manufacturer and purchased by the U.S. Army. Kedrin received Vasiliev's report, found it interesting, and asked for additional information about

Aeronautical Station Commander Lieutenant Dorozhinsky, the first Russian officer who received a pilot's license. In 1911, at his recommendation, an Antoinette landplane was fitted with floats at Sevastopol. It was the first Russian seaplane tested on the water. *Gennady Petrov Collection Photograph.*

Voisin *Canard* floatplane. Two machines of this type were purchased in France in 1912 and they became the first airplanes of the Imperial Russian Navy. *Gennady Petrov Collection Photograph.*

Curtiss seaplanes, which he received before leaving. The Russian officers planned to negotiate the purchase of Curtiss seaplanes (reportedly, Glenn Curtiss was in England at the time) and an Etrich airplane in Austria.

However, the plans were destined to fail. Kedrin could not meet Glenn Curtiss in England, and for some reason, it was not possible to buy Etrich airplanes; as a result, it was decided to sign an agreement with the French company Voisin for the supply of two *Canard* seaplanes. After the execution of the contract Kedrin returned to Sevastopol, while Dorozhinsky remained in France to watch the construction of the aircraft and attend flight training. By October it became evident that Voisin was very late in the manufacture of the aircraft. It was clear that the delivery deadline would be broken. Moreover, in October 1911 Dorozhinsky was injured in a flight accident, contact with him was lost, and the fleet command was unable to receive information on the actual situation of the agreement. All of this annoyed the Commander of the Black Sea Fleet, vice-admiral Ebegard, and resulted in recalling Dorozhinsky from France. Instead of him, Lieutenant Stakhovsky was sent to perform the duties of inspection and resolution of current issues.

Seek and Ye Shall Find

Stakhovsky was dismayed by Voisin's factory and by the company's conditions. Since he was an active person, he tried to find another firm, more reliable, which could supply seaplanes for the Russian Navy. Quite rapidly, through an aviation newspaper, he found the address of the French aviator Louis Paulhan, who represented Glenn Curtiss in France. He wrote to him and, after receiving the command's authorization, he agreed that Paulhan would show him Curtiss's Hydroaeroplane at Antibes. The demonstration took place at the beginning of February 1912. The flights were performed by Hugh Robinson. Stakhovsky really liked the aircraft, sent a report to Kedrin describing in detail its characteristics, its advantages, and recommended the purchase of three seaplanes: two two-seaters and one single-seater. The fleet command supported the proposal. At the end of February the contract for the supply of aircraft was signed by maritime agent Kartsev on behalf of the Russian fleet and by the director general, Jerome Fanciulli on behalf of the Curtiss Company.

Under the contract the first aircraft was to be delivered to France within a month, and the next two to Sevastopol within two months. It was agreed that spare parts and the engine were to be supplied simultaneously. Curtiss also undertook to send to Sevastopol a pilot and a mechanic to teach the staff of the naval base to fly and maintain Hydros. During the negotiations Lieutenant Stakhovsky obtained a significant discount, so the total amount of the contract was 100,000 francs.

Acceptance of the first consignment of Curtiss Hydros by the Commission of the Sevastopol Port, August 1912. Left to right: two members of the Commission, midshipman Utgoff, Lt. Stahovsky (seated on the float), midshipmen Essen and Kovedyaev (by the control wheel), Fride, Charles Witmer, Captain Kedrin, two members of the Commission, Doctor Pavlovsky. The airplane in the background was assigned fleet number 3. *Jerome S. Fanciulli Collection, History of Aviation Collection, Special Collections Department, McDermott Library, The University of Texas at Dallas.*

Subsequently, things were not so smooth. The first seaplane, that Stakhovsky expected in France, where he also hoped to attend a flight course run by Hugh Robinson, was not delivered on time. After competitions in Monaco, Robinson went to the USA; moreover, there were rumors that the aircraft destined for the Russian fleet had been sold to Italy, and Curtiss seriously risked having to pay a significant penalty. To conduct the business and solve the problem in its favor, the American firm engaged the owner of the trading company S.O. Ochs, who had a representative's office in Saint Petersburg. Long negotiations and correspondence started.

Meanwhile, work under the agreement continued. All three aircraft and the spare parts were sent from New York on two steamers, the first of which moored at Liepaja, a Russian port on the Baltic Sea, in the middle of May. Customs clearing took a rather long time, but finally the freight was sent by railway to Sevastopol, where it was delivered on July 1. Two Curtiss representatives, pilot Charles Witmer and mechanic George Hallett, were already waiting for it. Witmer flew the first aircraft, a two-seater Curtiss Model E, on August 11, 1912. The other two, Models E and D, were flown one month later, on September 11. According to the requirements, the aircraft had to demonstrate a flight endurance of one hour, a rate of climb of 300 meters in 9 minutes, carry 300 kg of useful load, and be able to take off and fly for 3 km with one engine cylinder inoperative.

The Commission of the Sevastopol port, established to receive the airplanes, was satisfied with the test results. The seaplanes were seaworthy enough, controllability afloat and in the air was decent, the aircraft were serviceable, and takeoff from water was also good. As a result, with insignificant remarks, all three aircraft were accepted. The two-seaters were assigned fleet numbers 3 and 4, and the single-seater was assigned number 5. Numbers 1 and 2 were destined for Voisin's *Canard* airplanes, which, although with delay, were delivered to Sevastopol in spring 1912.

"Curtisses" Start Working

As soon as the fleet accepted the Curtisses, Witmer began the training of Russian pilots. According to the contract, he had to train only one pilot, but there were seven candidates. All of them had already finished the courses at the Sevastopol Officer Pilot School, could fly land-based aeroplanes, and were young and enthusiastic, so the training was fast and soon they were all certified by Witmer for solo flight on the Curtisses. The first three aircraft were assigned to midshipmen Utgoff, Kovedyaev, and Essen.

While at Sevastopol the first batch of aircraft was being assembled and tested, Ochs signed the second contract with the Navy Ministry for the supply of three seaplanes. One model D and two model E Curtisses were manufactured and then delivered on time, and in November, after test flights, they were accepted by the commission of the port and assigned numbers 6, 7, and 8 respectively. Thus, by the end of 1912, at Sevastopol six Curtiss seaplanes were already in use. Charles Witmer, a direct participant in the events, described the flights and the Russian naval aviators around him:

> I have never met with men as a class who loved flying as these officers did. They flew at all times regardless of weather; they were in the air every minute of the time allowed them by the superior officer. In fact, it was only by the latter's good judgment that some serious accident was avoided. There was great rivalry between the navy flyers of the Black Sea Fleet stationed at Sevastopol and the army flyers who were stationed some forty minutes flight down the coast. It was the chief delight of the navy boys to fly to the army field and do stunts over the water were all could see. Sometimes they would return to Sevastopol flying overland. This was very dangerous as there were high cliffs and deep draws to pass over, up which strong gusts of wind blew, but the navy boys cared little about the dangers and flew over at every occasion. In this spirit, one of my pupils, Lieutenant Utgoff, flew a standard Curtiss to the military camp and gamboled up at the height of 5,250 feet for the benefit and envy of the army flyers.

Russian pilots liked the aircraft. The sailors appreciated Curtisses in all aspects and this allowed Ochs, with the support of the Commander of the Black Sea Fleet, vice-admiral Ebegard, in the beginning of December 1912, to settle the issue related to the penalty under the first contract.

Curtiss seaplanes were the first aircraft of the Russian fleet to be loaded on board a ship. In autumn 1912 a rigging device to lift an aircraft with a crane was tested. At the end of summer 1913 the collier *Dnepr* with Curtiss number 6 on board embarked from Sevastopol Bay and anchored 15 miles from the shore. On August 27 they tried twice to put the aircraft in the water, start the engine and take off. Both attempts failed; the take off did not succeed because, due to the waves, the engine and the air propeller became submerged. They lifted the aircraft on the deck and returned to the base. Despite the failure the sailors did not abandon the idea, and in the beginning of

Opposite
Top: Sailors beaching Curtiss number 3 Hydro, autumn 1912. Later on during its service life the canard was removed from the float and the airplane was fitted with rectangular upper wing tip extensions. The extensions were simply wing sections that were taken from the supply of spare parts. *Gennady Petrov Collection Photograph.*

Bottom: Imperial Russian Navy pilots: Fride (left), Zhukov (center) and Miklashevsky (right) together with seaplane base ground service personnel. Curtiss Hydro number 4 is in the background. *Gennady Petrov Collection Photograph.*

Above: Curtiss Hydroaeroplane number 8. It was delivered to Sevastopol with the second consignment of Curtiss airplanes and served up to the beginning of 1915. *Gennady Petrov Collection Photograph.*

Pilot Fride at the control wheel of Russian Curtiss number 3. *Gennady Petrov Collection Photograph.*

Above: First Russian fleet trials of using seaplanes launched from ships. Curtiss number 6 on the cathead of the collier *Dnepr*. Sevastopol, 1913. *Gennady Petrov Collection Photograph*.

Right: Curtiss number 5 preparing to board the cruiser *Kagul* during the trials of mid-1914. *Gennady Petrov Collection Photograph*.

1914 they made another series of experiments on loading and unloading the Curtiss from the ship, this time using the cruiser *Kagul*. On January 6 and January 22 seaplane No.5 was loaded on board. On February 6 the loading and unloading of two seaplanes simultaneously was perfected; Lieutenant Utgoff's No.5 and midshipman Ragozin's No.7. The required duration of operations gradually decreased, and in the end it took just a few minutes.

The archives of Sevastopol have preserved information according to which in August 1914 Utgoff and Ragozin were unloaded from the *Kagul* to the water on their Curtiss 60 miles from shore and flew to the air base at Kruglaya Bay, near Sevastopol. In September they took off from Kruglaya Bay and, after an hour-long reconnaissance flight, they landed on the *Kagul*. The experience was not wasted; because during World War I the Russian Black Sea Fleet used several aircraft carriers. They were equipped mainly with flying boats M-5 and M-9, which were used rather successfully to bomb Turkish seaports and to escort convoys.

Curtiss floatplanes were also used for other experiments that were very interesting at the time. In autumn 1912 Charles Witmer, by request of the Russian command, studied the effect of salvo fire from naval guns on the flight of an aeroplane. Flying in a Curtiss in a training area, at a height of 1,500 ft, he flew at a mile's distance in front of four ships which fired salvos at a target. He flew right above the fifth one, but to his surprise he did not notice any fluttering, neither in the air nor in the structure of the aeroplane. In the summer of 1913 attempts were made to equip a seaplane with a compass. The instrument made in Sevastopol was flawed, so another one was ordered in Saint Petersburg and mounted on Curtiss No.5. The tests were successful, the innovation turned out to be useful and with time, almost all Curtisses were equipped with a compass. In the beginning of 1914, No.7 was equipped for the first time with a bomb rack for a 40 lb bomb. On February 24, as an experiment, midshipman Ragozin dropped a landmine with a TNT charge in the sea on a hypothetical target made of empty barrels. The experiment was successful. By mid-1914 carrying bombs on seaplanes was common.

It Was an Obvious Success
On June 12, 1913, on the fleet's initiative, another contract for the supply of seaplanes, spare parts and engines was signed. Initially the contract was for three floatplanes. However Ochs, expecting further orders from Russia, proposed to replace one of them with a flying boat, at the price of a floatplane. The proposal was clearly profitable; flying boats had many advantages compared to Curtiss floatplanes, at least on paper, and the command approved the deal. In September the fleet accepted the last two Curtiss Hydros, numbered 9 and 10.

Another type of Curtiss floatplane was delivered to Russia as well. It was an amphibious aircraft, equipped with a retractable wheeled landing gear. Apparently

Top left: Curtiss number 7 aboard the cruiser *Kagul*, Sevastopol, 1914. This airplane also became the first Russian seaplane equipped with a bomb rack and subsequently it was used for bomb dropping tests in 1914. *Gennady Petrov Collection Photograph.*

Above: It was too cramped on the deck of the cruiser *Kagul*. Two Curtiss Hydroaeroplanes, numbers 7 and 5, are hardly discernible among the davits, rigging and other ship's equipment. *Gennady Petrov Collection Photograph.*

Below: In addition to the main contracts, this Curtiss Hydroaeroplane equipped with retractable landing gear had been delivered to Saint Petersburg for demonstration in mid-1912. Later it was taken to Sevastopol. *Gennady Petrov Collection Photograph.*

Bottom: Curtiss Hydro, Sikorsky S5A and Farman floatplane during the tests at Grebnoy port, Saint Petersburg, c.1912. *Gennady Petrov Collection Photograph.*

Opposite
Top: Russian Curtiss Hydroaeroplanes in a line at Kilen Bay Station. Sevastopol, c.1912-1913. *Gennady Petrov Collection Photograph.*

Bottom: Recovery operation of Curtiss number 5. *Gennady Petrov Collection Photograph.*

Ochs wanted to show the invention to the fleet command, and the aircraft was delivered to Saint Petersburg in mid-1912 for a demonstration. In the autumn of 1912 the amphibian was transported to Sevastopol, however there is no information available on its fate.

The Sevastopol air force detachment was a part of the Communication Service of the Black Sea Fleet. It was directed by Stakhovsky. The aeroplanes were based at Kilen Bay. The pilots trained mainly for reconnaissance of ships and submarines in the sea, and in 1913 they flew 235 hours on Curtisses. Curious cases happened as well. A prison-ship was anchored in the bay of Sevastopol. Charles Witmer was performing a reconnaissance flight with General Kalbash over the sea and noticed a lifeboat with five prisoners and two guards near the unusual vessel. On the way back, the general noticed the struggle in the lifeboat between the prisoners and the guards; from the height of 400 ft. he could see that the prisoners threw one guard overboard and shot another. Kalbash asked Witmer to fly the aircraft to the flagship where he told about the escape. Immediately several armed groups were sent to the place of the accident. Soon three dead prisoners were dispatched to the ship; it is not known where the other two disappeared.

Curtiss Model O engine on the test bench. These engines provided some problems for Russian pilots and mechanics because of their poor reliability. *Gennady Petrov Collection Photograph.*

Failures were frequent on the Curtisses. The aircraft constantly had do be repaired. The metallic parts, made of thin sheets, rusted in the salty water, and they had to be cleaned, painted or replaced. Wings often had to be re-covered; for this purpose, cloth had to be ordered from America. Damaged wooden parts were either repaired in the woodworking shop, or replaced with spare parts. But the main problems were caused by the engine. Cracks were found in the crankcases, and in the summer of 1913 a special commission was established to solve technical issues related to repair and re-commissioning of engines. In the middle of February 1914 the first Curtiss, No.4, was written off. It crashed during an emergency water landing in fog. The pilots, Lieutenant Utgoff and his trainee Tyufaev, survived. Two months later, again during a landing, the fleet lost aircraft No.6. It sank while it was being towed to the base by a torpedo boat.

In 1914 Curtiss Hydros started to be decommissioned, replaced by flying boats, which were more seaworthy and could lift heavier loads. They were equipped with Curtiss "OX" engines. The last Curtiss floatplane, No.9, was written off at the beginning of May 1915.

Between September and early November the first Curtiss flying boat was tested at Sevastopol. The aircraft had good characteristics, and it was accepted by the fleet, and numbered No.11. Almost immediately, at the end of 1913, a contract was made for the delivery of 6 flying boats. Thus, in a year and a half, Curtiss supplied 17 seaplanes to Russia. It was definitely a success by the standards of the time. New orders were being considered. Inspired by the prospects, in September 1913 Glenn Curtiss went to Saint Petersburg. The main purpose of his visit was to obtain a concession to open an airplane factory in Russia. It is not known why these plans were not fulfilled.

Two Curtiss Hydroaeroplanes in a line with Curtiss flying boats. Sevastopol, c.1913-1914. *Gennady Petrov Collection Photograph.*

"Just how badly the cruisers were damaged has never been ascertained, but it is a fact that neither of them ever returned"

At the outbreak of World War I the Russian Fleet had 25 airplanes. Baltic Sea and Liepaja served as a base for ten airplanes of various types: Farman, FBA and Sikorsky seaplanes. The air force detachment of the Black Sea Fleet Communication Service possessed 15 aircraft. Six Curtiss floatplanes, seven Curtiss flying boats and two Morane floatplanes were commissioned in various degrees of completion. By early October 1914 two other Curtiss seaplanes crashed during accidents, numbers 3 and 7. The remaining four aircraft were still based in Sevastopol Kilen Bay Station.

On October 14 Black Sea Headquarters received a message from the steamboat *Queen Olga,* notifying them that 5 miles from Bosphorus Strait it had met a group of German cruisers and destroyers. The next day another Russian trading vessel reported that one of the German ships, the cruiser *Goeben,* was discovered 140 miles to the

Curtiss flying boat sailing towards the seaplane station after a reconnaissance flight. Sevastopol, c.1914. *Gennady Petrov Collection Photograph.*

east of the Bosphorus. The cruiser was headed for Sevastopol. On October 16, at 3:20 a.m. Turkish destroyers broke through to the port of Odessa. At 4:48 a.m. all Russian Black Sea Fleet bases received the radio message: "The war has begun."

Goeben was the most powerful combat vessel on the Black Sea. It appeared at 4 nautical miles from Sevastopol accompanied by Turkish torpedo boats on the same day at 6:30 a.m. and brought down fire on the city. Coastal batteries immediately struck back. Junior Lieutenant Svetukhin was the first who took off in Hydro No.10, promptly found both *Goeben* and the torpedo boats, but the fleet's airplanes were not equipped for bomb-dropping yet, and the pilot could only watch enemy actions from the air. After that the flying boats took to the air. The exchange of fire continued for about twenty minutes. At 6:50 a.m. the cruiser stopped firing and broke off the fight. In total that day Russian pilots made about twenty reconnaissance flights. On October 16 in response to the attack on its Black Sea towns Russia declared a war on Turkey.

In November Sevastopol was again attacked by a German-Turkish squadron headed by the cruiser *Breslau*. By that time almost all Curtiss flying boats were equipped with bomb racks. The enemy's ships were quickly discovered, the airplanes promptly launched, now equipped with bombs. The Germans, now being attacked both from the sea and the air preferred to flee. Curtiss Hydro No.10 made only one reconnaissance flight that day.

Charles Witmer was the witness to these events again:

> Then seven flying boats – all of American make, delivered just before outbreak of the war – started, and circling over the two steamers as they proceeded in full retreat under full steam out of the harbor, dropped their bombs and hurried back to shore. This manoeuvre was carried out without a flaw, but while the machines were returning to shore for their second load of bombs, the cruisers had gained too many miles to make further damage of bombs possible, so the aeroplanes returned to shore after a long chase. Just how badly the cruisers were damaged has never been ascertained, but it is a fact that neither of them ever returned.

> After that initial success, the defence of the entire coast was left to the aeroplanes, and for three months, during my stay at Sevastopol, I saw them go out daily to reconnoiter. In this way, Russia was able, with an equipment of seven aeroplanes, costing about $100,000, to dispense with the service of several cruisers and to insure ample protection to Sevastopol from the German raiders.

Witmer probably slightly exaggerated the events, having combined in his narration the impressions of two attacks. According to historical data there was no bombardment during the first attack and for defeating the second one, only two Russian flying boats were sent and only one bomb was dropped. Nevertheless he is substantially right: German cruisers did not ever return.

Japan

Besides Russia, Curtiss seaplanes were purchased by navies of other countries, yet considerably less and comparatively little data remains about them.

In early 1912 the Imperial Japanese Navy's command decided to create its own air unit. Demonstration flights by W.B. Atwater in his Curtiss Hydro near Yokohama during May-June 1912 probably impressed navy personnel and the fleet sent its officers, including Lieutenant Sankichi Kono, to Hammondsport, NY to study flying and to purchase airplanes. At the same time another group of fleet representatives was sent to France for the same purpose. After a while Lt. Kono was recalled. He did not even have enough time to complete the flying training course. However, it was decided to purchase two Curtiss Model E seaplanes; they were delivered to Japan and Kono got off the water on his plane from the air station in Oppama (Yokosuka) on November 2, 1912. Therefore, the Curtiss Hydro became the first airplane in the Japanese fleet. The Grand Naval Review took place in Yokohama on November 12 and aircraft participated in it for the first time ever. Flights were carried out with Curtiss and Farman floatplanes. Two Maurice Farman machines were purchased in France and put into operation together with the Curtiss Hydros.

A number of new Curtiss Model E aircraft were manufactured in Japan. They were similar to the U.S. airplanes but they were designated as Type Ka seaplanes. The airplanes were mostly used for training and remained in the inventory until 1915. Lt. Chikuhei Nakajima, the future owner of an aircraft manufacturing company, built a unique airplane based on the Curtiss Hydro in 1913. The aircraft

Japanese delegation at Hammondsport posing with a Curtiss Hydroaeroplane. Left to right: Commander Shigetoshi Takeuchi, Japanese Naval Attaché at Japanese embassy in Washington, D.C., Lansing Callan, Chuji Yamada and Francis Wildman (at the control wheels), Harry Genung, Lieutenant Sankichi Kono (in light suit), Motohisa Kondo, Mr. Oliver and Chikuhei Nakajima, founder of the Nakajima Aircraft Co. September 1912. *U.S. Naval History and Heritage Command Photograph.*

was named Yokosho Experimental Navy-Type Seaplane. The first flight took place in the autumn. The aircraft was made as a single copy, and generally it was similar to the Curtiss Hydro design scheme, but was equipped with a Farman type pilot's nacelle and the ailerons were installed on the upper wings.

Italy

Société d'aviation Paulhan was given an order by the Italian Government for delivery of three Curtiss Hydroaeroplanes in late July 1912. The first aircraft was accepted by the Commission at Juan-les-Pins on September 1. Louis Paulhan, a representative of Curtiss in France, greatly facilitated the transaction and in Italy these aircraft were therefore often called Paulhan-Curtiss airplanes. All three Curtiss and two Borel seaplanes were delivered to the air base in Venice established in the early 1913. The detachment was then named San Marco. First it consisted of several pilots, including Ludovico De Filippi, one of the famous pioneers of Italian aviation. A flying school for navy pilots commanded by Lt. Ginocchio was formed of the detachment and the first trainees started exercising in the early February 1913.

Curtiss Hydros were chiefly used by the Italian Fleet for training purposes. However, these seaplanes took part in experiments, such as lifting an aircraft aboard a ship and putting it afloat. After the lifting device was put into service, Bruno Brivonesi, a graduate from the Venetian School of Pilots, made a round trip aboard the cruiser *Dante Alighieri,* visiting Italian seaport towns and performing test flights in his Curtiss during the stops.

No reliable information on additional purchases of Curtiss seaplanes in Italy has been found so far. The aircraft were taken out of service very quickly but the fleet was supplied with Curtiss flying boats during 1913-1914.

Italian aviator Ludovico De Filippi at the control wheel of his Curtiss Hydroaeroplane. *Courtesy of the Glenn H. Curtiss Museum, Hammondsport, NY.*

Germany

It is known that two Curtiss seaplanes were operated in Germany beginning in 1912. However, there are no details on that delivery as of today.

Civilians Fly the Hydroaeroplane

Curtiss Aeroplane Co. models and prices from a 1912-1913 sales brochure. *Courtesy of the Glenn H. Curtiss Museum, Hammondsport, NY.*

Opposite
Top: Al J. Engel seated on his Curtiss Hydroaeroplane, named *Bumble Bee*. A set of organ pipes is on the seat next to Engel. He is also reported to have carried a wireless radio. *Courtesy of the Western Reserve Historical Society, Cleveland, Ohio.*

Bottom: Al J. Engel flying his *Bumble Bee* over power boat races on the Niagara River at Buffalo, NY during the Commodore Perry Centennial celebrations in September 1913. The large ship in the background is the gunboat USS *Hawk* of the New York Naval Militia. *Courtesy of the Glenn H. Curtiss Museum, Hammondsport, NY.*

The Curtiss commercial product offerings gave the prospective owner or operator a rather wide selection of options from which to choose, including the size of the engine and the weight-lifting capability of the airframe. The hydroaeroplane floats and accessories were listed as a separate option. Refer to the "Models and Prices" illustration for details.

As early as 1911 the Curtiss Hydroaeroplane had been sold to individuals who used the airplanes for a variety of purposes, ranging from performing at air shows to carrying the mail. We do not know all of the owners and operators, only the more famous, most of whom were very interesting characters. All of them made an impression on the public, and they all participated in the advancement of aviation.

Al J. Engel

Engel, who was born in Cleveland, OH, was fascinated with motor sports and airplanes at an early age and left home to learn to fly at the Curtiss school in Hammondsport. He quickly became an excellent aviator, joined the Curtiss Exhibition Co., and toured the country with the team of Curtiss aviators. He earned enough money on the air show tour to purchase his own Curtiss biplane, which he later traded in for a used Curtiss Hydroaeroplane. Engel quit the Curtiss Exhibition Co. in 1912 and flew his Hydro to Cleveland, where he hoped to make a living with his machine. Engel created a contest, for ladies only, to name his new plane. The name *Bumble Bee* was chosen and the winner received a free flight.

Engel based the airplane at the Lakewood Yacht Club and tried all sorts of schemes to profit from the public's fascination with airplanes. He carried many passengers on their first airplane rides, participated in air shows, and started an aerial photography business. In the summer of 1913 he flew demonstrations at the centennial celebrations for Commodore Perry's victory over the British fleet on Lake Erie in the War of 1812. In the summer of 1914 he started a mail route on Chautauqua Lake, NY, receiving official U.S. airmail route number 607,004. He was only allowed to carry postcards on the route, but he also carried passengers on tours of the lake during the summer.

The *Bumble Bee* was a unique airplane at the time, having a one-off Curtiss Model O engine named the "Odd O" because of its higher horsepower rating compared to the standard Model O engine. Engel's Curtiss hydroaeroplane is the only one to have survived the 100 years since it was built in Hammondsport. It is currently on display at the Crawford Auto-Aviation Museum in Cleveland.

Engel returned to work for Curtiss in 1915 as a flight instructor and remained with the company until the start of World War I, when he started his own aircraft

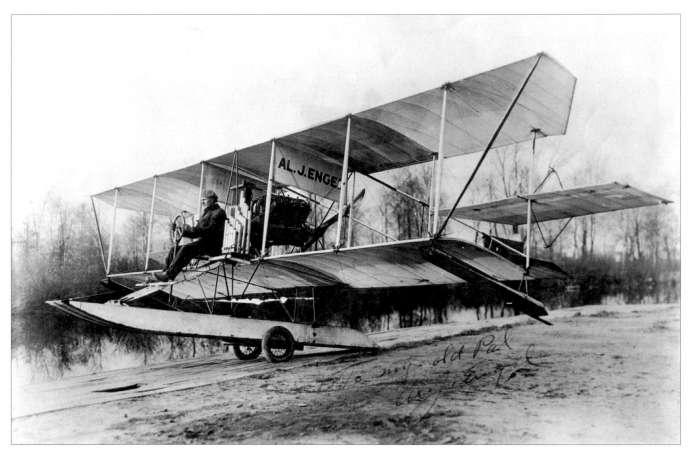

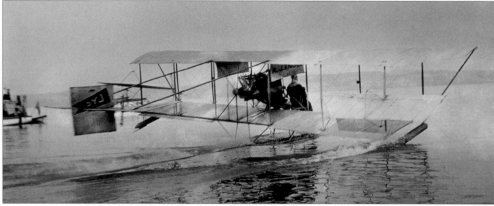

Above: Curtiss Pilots Al J. Engel (left) and William Hoff at the January 1912 Dominguez Hills air meet near Los Angeles. Hoff was seriously injured the following month at an air meet in Oakland, CA. *Courtesy of University of Southern California, on behalf of the USC Special Collections, photo CHS-11684.*

Top right: Al. J. Engel preparing for takeoff in his Curtiss Hydroaeroplane, named *Bumble Bee*. The symbol painted on the rudder is the red, white, and blue burgee of the Lakewood Yacht Club, where Engel based his flying activities. *Courtesy of the Western Reserve Historical Society, Cleveland, Ohio.*

manufacturing company. The company built training airplanes for the Army during the war and after the war it modified airplanes to carry the mail. The business soon failed and he returned to Curtiss where he became manager of one of the plants in Buffalo, NY. During World War II he came out of retirement and became general manager of the National Aircraft Co., a manufacturer of gliders. Al J. Engel passed away in 1979 at the age of 99.

Terah T. Maroney

One of the more colorful aviators of his time, Terah T. Maroney, or more commonly called T.T. Maroney, was born in Murfreesboro, TN on March 7, 1880. He grew up in Huntsville, AL, where he became a cabinetmaker. In 1908 he moved to Montana, where he worked in the construction industry. During 1910 he became interested in aviation and built an airplane in his spare time. He made several flights in Great Falls with the airplane before destroying it in a takeoff accident. He spent all of his savings on the airplane but he managed to scrape together enough money to build a second airplane of his own design.

Maroney used the second airplane to fly at exhibitions where he earned enough money to attend the Curtiss School in San Diego. He graduated from the school in March 1912 and was awarded license no. 106. There were 13 students in Maroney's class at the Curtiss School, and by October 1913 seven had been killed in airplane accidents. Of the remaining six, only two were still flying. He returned to Montana where he convinced a group of Butte businessmen to form the Montana Aeroplane and Exhibition Company with Maroney as their pilot. A second-hand Model E with a 75-hp Model O engine was purchased from The Curtiss Aeroplane Co. and delivered in August 1912.

T.T. Maroney sitting with female pilot on pontoon of Curtiss pusher, Lake Washington, Seattle, c.1915. *Courtesy of the Montana Historical Society Research Center-Photograph Archives, Helena, Montana, Photo PAC 79-36.296a.*

Maroney made many exhibition flights with the new Curtiss during the years 1912 through early 1914, employing stunts like dropping sacks of flour to simulate a bombing. He even persuaded a young woman named Ruby Rutledge to parachute from his airplane. The Montana State legislature was so impressed with one of Maroney's flying exhibitions that they named him the "official aviator" of Montana.

T.T. Maroney with co-pilot behind dual control wheel Curtiss pusher airplane, Seattle; co-pilot is Eddie Hubbard; c.1915. Courtesy of the Montana Historical Society Research Center-Photograph Archives, Helena, Montana, Photo PAC 79-36-300.

In 1914 he moved his flight operations to Seattle, WA, where he added floats to the airplane and began a flying school and charter company, taking passengers on flights over the city. One of his passengers was William Boeing, the founder of the Boeing Company. Boeing was interested in aeronautics but had not yet flown on an airplane, when on July 4, 1914 he flew with Maroney on a flight over Lake Washington. He was thoroughly impressed with the flying experience but was not so thrilled about the little Curtiss seaplane. Boeing told his friend Conrad Westervelt "I think we can build a better one." Westervelt, a lieutenant in the U.S. Navy and an assistant Naval Constructor, did a structural analysis of Maroney's airplane and concluded, "There isn't any reason this thing should hold together. The strength of the parts is just about equal to the load they have to carry." The rest, as they say, is history; Boeing and Westervelt went on to build their first airplane, the B&W, which flew in 1916.

In 1916 Maroney convinced the Washington State legislature to create an aeronautical section of the state's naval militia, and he was commissioned a lieutenant in the militia in April 1916. When the U.S. declared war on Germany in 1917, he signed on with the Army as a flight instructor at Gerstner Field, LA, where the Army had a Curtiss Hydroaeroplane in its inventory. Maroney was working for the Travel-Air Company in 1929 when he was hit in the head by the propeller he was cranking on a company airplane. He died two hours later in a hospital.

Hugh Robinson

A native of Neosho, MO, Hugh Robinson played a very important role in the development of the Curtiss Hydroaeroplane. He was one of Glenn Curtiss's most trusted colleagues and was a close friend. At an early age he was recognized as a risk-taker, parachuting from hot air balloons and performing other daring exploits. After building his own glider in 1904 and crashing it, he moved on to build a dirigible balloon in 1907. He built a 40hp engine to power the dirigible, but it was not a complete success because the engine was not powerful enough to support the dirigible.

Louis Paulhan, the famous French aviator and the Curtiss Company's sales representative in Europe. He is shown here on the first Curtiss-Paulhan Hydroaeroplane. © *Musée de l'Air et de l'Espace/Paris-Le Bourget Photo 71 079.*

Louis Paulhan

Glenn Curtiss first met the famous French aviator, Louis Paulhan at the Rheims air meet in 1909, in which Paulhan won third place in the endurance test by flying his Voisin for 2 hours and 43 minutes. He was born in 1883 in Pézenas, France, and at seventeen he enlisted in the French Army and became a balloon pilot. During his spare time he experimented with model airplanes, and in 1908 one of his models won a contest sponsored by the Aero Club of France. The prize was a real Voisin airplane, minus the engine. He obtained a 7-cylinder Gnome rotary engine, installed it in the airplane and proceeded to teach himself how to fly.

Paulhan was quick to master the art of flying, and by the summer of 1909 he had participated in several exhibitions in France, winning many of the events. In the Rheims event he competed in the Grand Prix endurance event, the speed trials, and the altitude event in which he and his Voisin achieved an altitude of 295 ft. In total his winnings amounted to 10,000 Francs, about one third of the money that had been won by Curtiss. Paulhan's aerial exploits at Rheims were marred by a near collision with Leon Delagrange in his Bleriot, which resulted in Paulhan crashing his airplane.

In early 1910 at the air meet at Dominguez, near Los Angeles, Paulhan took the majority of the prize money offered in these events:

Height: $3,000, 4,165 feet, first place
Endurance and Time: $3,000, 75.77 miles, 1:52:32, first place
Speed, 10 laps: $2,000, 16.11 miles, 24:59 2/5, second place
Three laps, with passenger: $3,000, 4:83 miles, only entrant
Cross-country: $10,000, first place

Paulhan's Farman biplane was much larger than the Curtiss entries and easily took the prizes for height, endurance and the cross-country event. The Curtiss airplanes excelled in the speed events and the quick-start trials. After the events at Dominguez, Paulhan barnstormed his way back to New York, giving exhibitions to large crowds, while fighting off the Wright brothers' lawyers who were attempting to stop him from performing due to alleged patent infringement.

Finally rid of the Wrights' lawyers and back in Europe, Paulhan used his reliable long-distance-flying Farman machine to capture the £10,000 prize for the first flight

Hugh Robinson's rebuilt Hydroaeroplane on the launch/recovery ramp at Monaco, circa 1912.© *Musée de l'Air et de l'Espace/Paris-Le Bourget, Photo MC 8220.*

between London and Manchester. The *Daily Mail* offered the prize to the first aviator to fly between the two cities within 24 hours. To get a head start on his competitor, Claude Grahame-White, Paulhan completed a risky night flight, arriving in Manchester on the morning of April 28, 1910.

Having earned large sums of money from his exhibitions and the London-Manchester prize, Paulhan started his own airplane company, producing a few prototypes. The two machines incorporated many new and innovative features but did not attract buyers. Shortly thereafter, as noted in the previous section, Paulhan became the European sales agent for Curtiss and assembled Curtiss airplanes from kits that were shipped to him by the Curtiss factory in Hammondsport.

Paulhan entered a Curtiss-Paulhan hydroaeroplane in several air meets during 1912, attracting the attention of military representatives who were assessing their war-fighting needs for the impending war in Europe. He sold several Curtiss-Paulhan hydroaeroplanes to European governments and a few to individuals. When war broke out in Europe in 1914, he joined the French Army as a fighter pilot and was decorated for his service on the Serbian front. After the war he worked in the French aircraft industry before retiring. Louis Paulhan died in 1963 at the age of 79.

William B. Atwater

Born William Bull Atwater on June 20, 1881, Bill Atwater was undoubtedly one of the more interesting owners of the Curtiss Hydroaeroplane. Bill lived in Central Valley, NY where he became an expert on the workings of automobile engines. He served in the Navy for seven years as a seaman and during the Spanish-American War, worked on a dispatch boat that sailed between Hong Kong and Manila. After his Navy service he worked on the steamship *St. Paul* as an assistant engineer.

Returning to Central Valley, he became deputy superintendent of roads for the city, and in late 1911 he eloped with a wealthy widow, Lillian Janeway Platt, who had been married to New York Senator Thomas Platt. Both of the Atwaters were interested in aviation, and they decided to go to California to take flying lessons. On the train trip to California they met Glenn Curtiss who persuaded them to come with him to San Diego and attend his flying school. Bill learned to fly very quickly, but Lillian apparently was happy just to fly with Bill as a passenger on one of the Curtiss Hydros. On a couple of occasions she carried a large net with her and snagged an unwary seagull.

The Atwaters obtained three Curtiss airplanes, two Hydros and one landplane and set off on a tour around the world with their new machines. In May 1912 the Atwaters arrived in Japan where Bill made a series of demonstration flights for Japanese government officials at Yokohama. On June 1 he conducted the first airmail

The affable William B. Atwater in a Curtiss Model D at the Dominguez Hills Air Meet, 1912. He set an American speed record of 73.08 mph at the meet. *Courtesy of University of Southern California, on behalf of the USC Special Collections, photo CHS-11722.*

William B. Atwater at the controls of his Curtiss Hydroaeroplane at the Curtiss camp, San Diego, CA, c.1911. *U.S. Naval History and Heritage Command Photograph NR&L (MOD) 29936.*

flight in Japan, carrying 1,000 letters and messages from Tokyo Mayor Kazuo Ozaki from the Shibaura port of Tokyo to Yokohama. It is not known if Glenn Curtiss was involved in funding the trip, but it certainly made good publicity for the Curtiss Aeroplane Co., and several Curtiss airplanes were subsequently sold to the Japanese Navy.

By November 1912 the Atwaters had moved on to Shanghai where they gave more flying demonstrations in front of very large crowds. They flew additional demonstrations in Singapore before arriving in Manila in March 1913 and later spent some time in Australia before heading back to the U.S., arriving in New York in April 1913. The Atwaters were paid for some of their exhibitions, but they donated some of their winnings to charity. The expenses for the trip were very high, and in 1914 he declared bankruptcy and was incarcerated for a short period because he refused to disclose how much money he had earned on his around-the-world junket.

Atwater became a flying instructor at the Wright school Augusta, GA in 1915, and when war was declared he joined the Navy again and was commissioned as a Naval Aviator, rated as Lieut. (j.g.). In February, 1918 he was appointed commandant of the U.S. detachment at a joint U.S.-Italian training facility near Bolsena, Italy where he trained American and Italian pilots, using Italian seaplanes. After the war he remained in the Naval Reserve and flew missions in the search for bootleggers during the Prohibition Era. (He himself was charged in 1929 for smuggling whiskey from Bimini to Florida.)

The Atwaters separated in 1927 and divorced in 1932. Bill worked for a few airlines in the twenties and became a test pilot for the American Aeronautical Company that was importing Savoia-Marchetti seaplanes into the U.S. In August 1930 he set an endurance record for seaplanes, flying a Savoia-Marchetti S.56 seaplane for over 22 hours. He worked for a few Central American airlines in the 1930s and died of a heart attack in New York City in January 1937.

Clair G. Horton

Born in 1890 in Pulteney, NY, about 10 miles from Hammondsport, Horton started working for Curtiss's motorcycle company as a teenager. Before learning to fly he was an airplane and engine mechanic for the famous exhibition pilot Jimmie Ward. At one of Ward's exhibitions in Canada, Horton became friends with a Winnipeg businessman, William J. Robertson. In 1914 Robertson and Horton formed a partnership, purchased two used biplanes from Curtiss and went into business in Manitoba, using one airplane as a land plane, flying from Winnipeg Exhibition

Grounds, and the other as a hydroaeroplane based at Victoria Beach, a summer resort on Lake Winnipeg.

The business plan as stated by Robertson was to organize aviation classes under the direction of Horton and carry passengers on scenic flights. Horton had just recently become a pilot, and he flew the hydroaeroplane. Another pilot, the Englishman F.F. Minchin, was hired to fly the land plane. By the end of June 1914 both airplanes were ready for use. The rates for passengers were $3.00 for a flight in the morning and $10.00 in the afternoon. The tuition fee for student pilots was $400.00.

On July 13, Horton and his passenger, Dr. Atkinson of Selkirk, Manitoba, took off from the water near the pier at Winnipeg Beach. Almost immediately Horton found that he had no control of the elevator because he had neglected to release the gust lock on the cable. As he reached behind him to release the lock, the airplane pitched up and stalled, rolled to the right, and splashed into the lake. Dr. Atkinson received a severe gash on his right arm, and the plane was badly damaged. A canoe was sent out from the shore to rescue the men, who were clinging to the main float. With one aircraft out of service and the other not much in demand, the firm of Robertson and Horton decided to move out of Canada. At the end of August, the partners and their two machines went south to Detroit Lakes, MN where they flew for the rest of the season.

Horton's flying career lasted less than a year, during which time he survived two splashes in his hydroaeroplane. Returning to a job that used his expertise as a mechanic, he joined the Philadelphia Aviation School 1916 at Essington as a mechanic/instructor. During the war he served as civilian instructor for the military. He stayed on as a civilian instructor for the Army, moved to Texas and served 43 years as an industrial engineer, mostly at Kelly Field in San Antonio. Clair Horton passed away in September 1963 at the age of 72.

Flugzeugbau Friedrichshafen GmbH

After the May 1912 Aero Show in New York Glenn Curtiss asked one of his pilots, Charles Witmer, to deliver a new Hydro to a customer in Germany. The trip was supposed to last nine weeks, but Witmer actually stayed in Europe for more than one year, delivering Curtiss airplanes in Austria, France, Germany, and Russia. One of the German customers was Flugzeugbau Friedrichshafen GmbH, a newly formed airplane manufacturing company located near the Zeppelin factory on the Bodensee (Lake Constance). The company began operations in 1912 and was partially funded by Zeppelin.

Witmer delivered the airplane to the company's chief engineer, Theodor Kober, who designed the original airship for Count Zeppelin. Kober was interested in building his own series of hydroaeroplanes and therefore purchased the Curtiss machine for use as a means of understanding the design and operation of water borne aircraft. One potential use of hydroaeroplanes envisioned by Kober was for the protection of the fleet of Zeppelins that would soon be involved in warfare. The protection scheme that was envisioned incorporated a small platform on top of the Zeppelin to allow a Triad-type hydroaeroplane to take off and engage attacks from enemy aircraft. In addition to the platform, a small streamlined hangar was to be incorporated.

To test the compatibility of an airplane with a Zeppelin, Witmer was asked to fly the Hydro in formation with one of the Zeppelins, the *Viktoria Luise*. Witmer was very impressed with the size of the Zeppelin and commented "I never appreciated the size of these leviathans of the air until I flew alongside that ship. It was like rowing past an ocean liner in a small skiff; the sides stretched ahead of me as far as I could see, and towered above me like a cliff." Witmer flew directly above the *Viktoria Luise* for a short time and became convinced that an airplane could easily land on a Zeppelin when it was moving through the air. Apparently nothing came of the scheme although the idea popped up periodically in the popular press after the war.

Shortly after Witmer left Friedrichshafen, Kober modified the Curtiss flight control system to the one on which he had been trained to fly in Germany. Apparently Kober had some difficulties in controlling the Hydro and requested Witmer's assistance as an experienced flight test pilot. When Witmer realized that the flight control system had been modified, he refused to fly the Hydro. Kober then hired the noted Swiss test pilot, Robert Gsell to do the flight-testing.

Gsell arrived in Friedrichshafen and soloed in the Curtiss on November 5, 1912. He was not impressed with the airplane's longitudinal flight characteristics, comparing it to running a hurdle race. This particular Hydro was equipped with both the front and rear elevators, which might have contributed to the longitudinal instability. Another problem encountered by Gsell was the breakage of propellers caused by their impacting the main float's wake. He was able to overcome that problem by carefully applying power while on the water.

The little Curtiss proved to be a valuable laboratory tool for Flugzeugbau Friedrichshafen, both from a design standpoint and from an operational aspect. Having learned to fly the Curtiss Hydro, Gsell successfully flew the company's first airplane, the FF.1 later in November 1912. The FF.1 was similar in layout to the Curtiss Hydroaeroplane, but it incorporated the lessons learned from the operation of the Curtiss. A small float under the horizontal tail was added to help keep the propeller from striking the water during takeoff and landing. The two-man crew was enclosed in a pod in a tandem arrangement, but other than those changes, the FF.1 looked very similar to the Curtiss Hydro. Even the tail struts were fabricated from bamboo!

Flugzeugbau Friedrichshafen went on to build many seaplanes and land planes for the German forces during World War I, and after the war they were taken over by the Dornier Company, which became a successful aircraft manufacturer of seaplanes and land planes.

Curtiss Aviation Schools

Curtiss operated several aviation schools that offered training on the Hydroaeroplane as well as on land planes. The original school, which was located at San Diego on North Island, began operating in early 1911, shortly after the invention of the hydroaeroplane. Given the seasonal nature of the weather in Hammondsport, the operation of the school there was supplemented by Curtiss schools in Miami and San Diego. The Miami school opened in January 1912 under the leadership of Charles Witmer, who had just returned from his European tour of duty.

By 1915 the Model F flying boats had replaced the Hydroaeroplane as the seaplane primary trainer, so it is probable that only the military was flying the Hydroaeroplane from 1915 forward. In the fall of 1915 Curtiss sponsored the Atlantic Coast Aeronautical Station in Newport News, VA, led by his old friend Thomas Scott Baldwin. Many of the civilian students and instructors, including Canadians, later became famed World War I flyers. Victor Carlstrom, Vernon Castle, Eddie Stinson and Gen. Billy Mitchell trained there.

The Curtiss Hydroaeroplane was one of the first airplanes to be sold to individuals and in its brief period of existence it provided a good platform for the training of water flyers around the world. The people listed above represent only a fraction of the aviators who flew the Curtiss Hydroaeroplane.

Below: One of the two Curtiss training aircraft at the Curtiss Aviation School in Miami, FL, c.1912. The other aircraft was a land plane. *Courtesy State Archives of Florida, Photo PR00454.*

Bottom: The Miami School's chief pilot, Charles Witmer is shown here carrying a student pilot to the Curtiss Hydroaeroplane. *Courtesy State Archives of Florida, Photo PR00483.*

A 1912 magazine advertisement for the newly-opened Curtiss Aviation School at Miami, FL. *Aero, America's Aviation Weekly, January 13, 1912.*

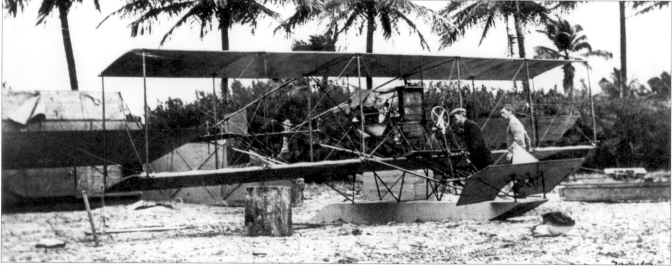

The Curtiss Hydroaeroplane in Detail

Primary Curtiss Hydro Versions

Curtiss Hydroaeroplanes were produced at the Curtiss Aeroplane Co. plant in Hammondsport and were delivered in the period from 1911 to 1916. The general arrangement scheme of the airplane was practically unchanged during this time. It was a three-strut, single float pusher biplane with a propeller mounted immediately behind the wings, with fully open pilots' seating and truss-type tail booms made of bamboo. However, owing to further developments of Glenn Curtiss himself and his employees, the design of the Hydroaeroplane underwent serious changes in its details during these five years.

Curtiss Model E Hydro of 1911

The two-seat Curtiss Model E Hydroaeroplane that appeared in the summer of 1911 should probably be considered as the basic version of the aircraft. By this time the design of the aircraft in Glenn Curtiss's aviation camp at San Diego was more or less finalized and had acquired its customary appearance. The most specific distinction of this airplane from its later versions was a front elevator, or "canard", mounted on the nose of the main float. The upper and lower wings had the same span, 28 ft and 8 inches. Another specific feature of the airplane was the dimensions of the wing chord

A typical Curtiss 1911 Model E Hydro, with the front elevator on the nose of the main float, shown during takeoff. *Courtesy of the Glenn H. Curtiss Museum, Hammondsport, NY.*

Flying over Lake Keuka. A Model E Hydro version of 1912-1913 with the trapezoidal upper wing tip extensions and with forward elevator removed. *Courtesy of the Glenn H. Curtiss Museum, Hammondsport, NY.*

and the gap between the upper and lower planes. They were absolutely equal and were all 60 inches. The ailerons did not yet have the extended chord forward of the aileron hinge line. The airplane was equipped with a 75-h.p. Curtiss Model O engine. The fuel tank was mounted above the engine, under the upper wing center section. In total, that was the appearance of the most famous Model E Hydro, the first U.S. Navy airplane, delivered in July of 1911, and known as the A-1.

Curtiss Model E Hydro of 1912-13

In the autumn of 1912 Curtiss removed the "canards" from all of his pushers; both from landplanes and seaplanes. There is a legend, stating that during one of his air shows Lincoln Beachey crushed the front elevator when landing in his Curtiss landplane, and, so as not to lose money, decided to remove the damaged parts and continue his flights. Surprisingly, the aircraft, after a "modernization" like that, turned out to be more energetic and pleasant to control. This news reached Glenn Curtiss, who never installed "canards" on his airplanes after that. Another specific distinction of the 1912-13 version was the addition of trapezoidal wing tip extensions that provided the aircraft with more lifting-surface area. Ailerons with increased chord forward of the aileron hinge line were added. The aft part of the float was cut off sharply instead of being rounded. Two fuel tanks were then mounted on the engine bed, on both sides of the engine, instead of one tank under the upper wing. The engine remained the same, a Curtiss Model O; however; later on, it was at times replaced with the more advanced 90-h.p. Curtiss OX version.

Curtiss Model E Hydro of 1914-15

Starting in 1914 Curtiss Hydroaeroplanes were supplied only to the U.S. Navy. The aircraft featured a much larger main float, which provided for enhanced water-borne capabilities; the wing primary structure was reinforced, and the surface areas of the rudder and elevators were increased. Instead of the welded canister type wing tip floats, the wing tip floats from the Curtiss flying boats were installed, which had a light framework of wood, lined with rubberized fabric. The fuel tank was moved back under the upper wing section. The aircraft was equipped with 90-h.p. Curtiss OX engines (later OX-2) and T-shaped radiators with increased frontal surface area.

The following is a description of the Curtiss 1912 Model E Hydroaeroplane design.

Power Plant

The airplane was equipped with a four-stroke cycle, eight-cylinder V-type Curtiss Model O water-cooled engine with rated horsepower of 75-h.p. The stroke was 5 inches and the bore was 4 inches. The engine was fitted with a Schebler Model L carburetor and a Bosch DR8 magneto. After the beginning of World War 1 later engine modifications, such as the Curtiss OX-2, began to be equipped with Zenith carburetors and Berling magnetos, since deliveries from Germany were no longer possible. Two fuel tanks of welded thin metal sheet contained some 26 gallons of fuel. An El Arco (Livingston) radiator was used. The volume of water contained in the water cooling system was 4.6 gallons. Water circulation was provided by a pump installed on the engine shaft. The two-bladed wooden 7 ft-6 inch diameter propeller had a pitch of 5 ft-4 inches. The tips of the blades were sheathed in brass. The power plant could also include a hand-starting crank, connected with the engine shaft by means of a ratchet clutch. The handle of the starting crank was above and behind the pilots' seats, allowing the pilots to start the engine without assistance, even when the aircraft was on the water.

The engine, fuel tanks, radiator and starting crank were mounted on the engine bed, which was, in fact, a pair of three-layer wooden laminated beams, made of spruce and ash. The engine was fastened with six 3/8 inch bolts. The radiator was mounted in front of the engine, fastened also with bolts and fixed with two steel tube braces. Fuel tanks, as a rule, were located to the right and to the left from the engine. The earlier versions featured one fuel tank, which was mounted above the engine, under the upper wing center section. That arrangement was restored in the process of manufacturing the later versions of Curtiss Hydroaeroplanes. Gasoline was supplied to the carburetor via gravity flow and that is why the height of the intake fuel-air mixture Y-pipe to the cylinders varied depending on the tank(s) location. The engine bed was installed between central sections of the upper and lower wings by means of braces made of 3/4 inch and 1 inch steel tubes, forming a rigid truss work in the planes of the forward and aft spars of the center wing sections. Longitudinal loads were carried by two forward diagonal beams, connecting the main float, the forward spar of the lower wing central section and the engine bed beams.

The engine was controlled by means of cables from the pedals located on pilots' footrest. Left pedals of the pilots were used for throttle control; right pedals were used to control spark advance control system. Some of the aircraft had no spark

Left: The Curtiss Hydro power plant. This photo was taken from a 1912 advertisement, and it is significantly retouched, nevertheless all of the power plant assembly including the Model O engine, including radiator, starting crank and fuel tank are clearly visible. *Courtesy of the Glenn H. Curtiss Museum, Hammondsport, NY.*

Right: The Curtiss Model O engine assembly line at Hammondsport. *Courtesy of the Glenn H. Curtiss Museum, Hammondsport, NY.*

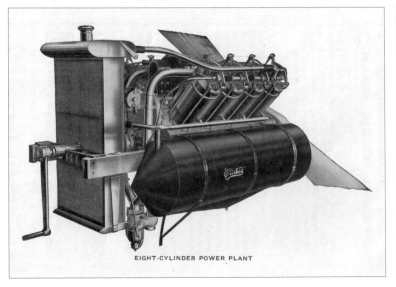

EIGHT-CYLINDER POWER PLANT

advance control system, so the pilots had only throttle control pedals on the footrest. The magneto starting pushbutton was usually installed on the steering column and was connected to the magneto with an electric wire, passing along the left forward diagonal beam.

Airplane Structure

Wing Biplane Box

The lower and upper wings each consisted of five separate sections, which permitted packing the disassembled aircraft in comparatively small crates for transportation. The upper wing was additionally equipped with trapezoidal wing tip extensions. Each section's framework was an assembly of spars and ribs made from laminated spruce. The stringers were installed to add rigidity to the structure, by forming in the area between the set of end ribs a structure in the form of divergent rays. Wing spars, ribs and stringers were connected to each other by means of metal plates, bent from light-gauge sheet metal. Forward and aft wing spars of the wing center sections (in the area of the engine installation) were made of laminated ash. The panels were joined using a bolted fastening system by means of connecting fittings, cut and bent of 1/16 inch sheet metal. Wing struts were made of laminated spruce. The wires bracing in the area of the wing midsections were doubled up, but were single in the area of outboard sections. Goodyear rubberized fabric was used for covering the wing. Fabric was glued to the frame and also hammered down with small wide head nails; a fabric strip was then glued on top of nails. The tail unit of the hydroaeroplane was covered in the same way. Al Engel's *Bumble Bee* aircraft had its fabric nailed down to the framework using rattan strips.

Some original parts of Curtiss Hydroaeroplanes are still kept at Hammondsport, in the Glenn Curtiss Museum. This is a Curtiss-produced wing panel of a Model D, showing its distinctive framework. The Model E panels had a similar design, but were somewhat larger in size. *Taras Chayka Photo Collection.*

Tail Unit and Ailerons

The rudder, stabilizer, elevators and ailerons were of similar design, and were made of solid spruce, while the most critical parts, such as the stabilizer spar were laminated. The framework parts (spars, ribs and stringers), the same as wing, were butt-joined together using light-gauge metal sheet plates. To provide rigidity to the aileron between its A-shaped bent steel tube control arm, the spar and trailing edge were braced with wires. Rigidity of the stabilizer and stability of the rudder position were achieved by means of a wire bracing system, stretched between these parts. The stabilizer angle of incidence could be adjusted when on the ground between zero to +4 degrees.

Left: Detail showing the joint composed of the front spar, end rib and the diagonal stringer. *Taras Chayka Photo Collection.*

Right: A close-up view of the stringers and rib joint. *Taras Chayka Photo Collection.*

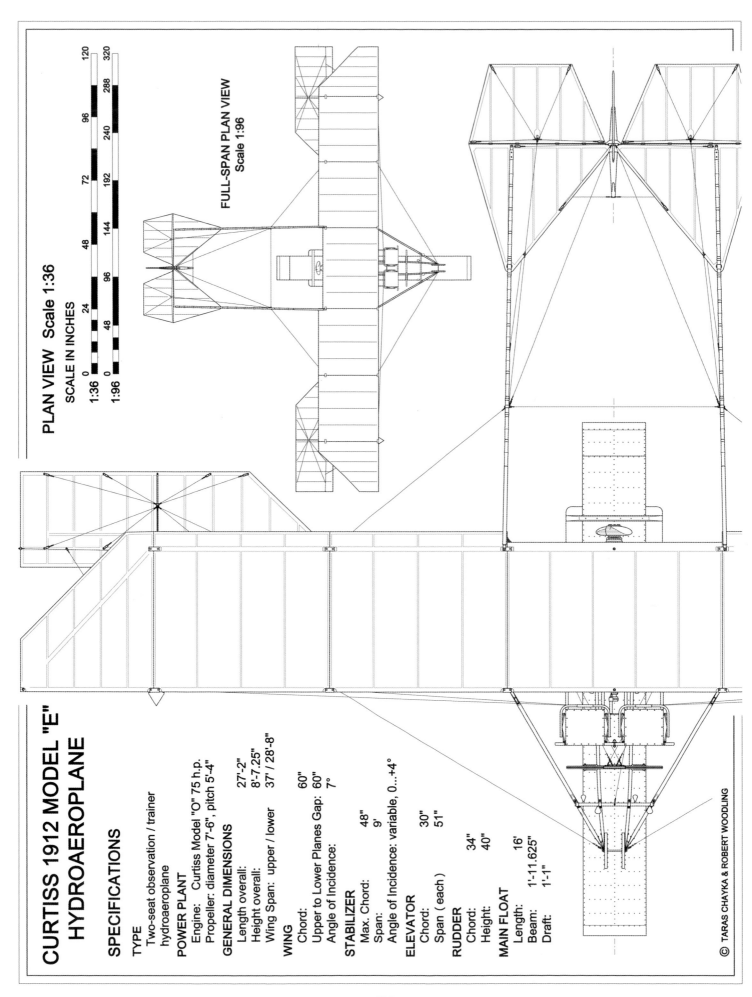

CURTISS 1912 MODEL "E" HYDROAEROPLANE

SPECIFICATIONS

TYPE
Two-seat observation / trainer hydroaeroplane

POWER PLANT
Engine: Curtiss Model "O" 75 h.p.
Propeller: diameter 7'-6", pitch 5'-4"

GENERAL DIMENSIONS
Length overall: 27'-2"
Height overall: 8'-7.25"
Wing Span: upper / lower   37' / 28'-8"

WING
Chord: 60"
Upper to Lower Planes Gap: 60"
Angle of Incidence: 7°

STABILIZER
Max. Chord: 48"
Span: 9'
Angle of Incidence: variable, 0...+4°

ELEVATOR
Chord: 30"
Span (each)   51"

RUDDER
Chord: 34"
Height: 40"

MAIN FLOAT
Length: 16'
Beam: 1'-11.625"
Draft: 1'-1"

PLAN VIEW   Scale 1:36

SCALE IN INCHES

1:36   0   24   48   72   96   120
1:96   0   48   96   144   192   240   288   320

FULL-SPAN PLAN VIEW
Scale 1:96

© TARAS CHAYKA & ROBERT WOODLING

126

CURTISS 1912 MODEL "E" HYDROAEROPLANE

SIDE VIEW Scale 1:36

SPECIFICATIONS (Continued)

AREAS

Wing total:	312.74 sq.ft
Aileron (total)	51.66 sq.ft
Stabilizer:	19.10 sq.ft
Elevator (total)	17.08 sq.ft
Rudder:	9.44 sq.ft

WEIGHTS

Empty:	990 lb
Gross:	1550 lb

PERFORMANCE

Speed:	60 mph
Climb Rate:	300 ft/min
Endurance:	4 h

NOTES

The configuration of the Curtiss Model E Hydroaeroplane was not fully standardized in 1912, and most of the airplanes of this type differed from each other in their detailed parts. The particular airplane chosen for this three-view drawing is U.S. Navy's A-3, as it was configured during 1912-1913. The A-3 was renamed AH-3 in 1914.

These drawings were made for use by aviation historians and modellers and should not be used for making full-scale operating airplanes

Drawings were scaled from museum articles and other sources.

Drawn by Taras Chayka, 2010.

FRONT VIEW Scale 1:36

SCALE IN INCHES

1:36   0   24   48   72   96   120

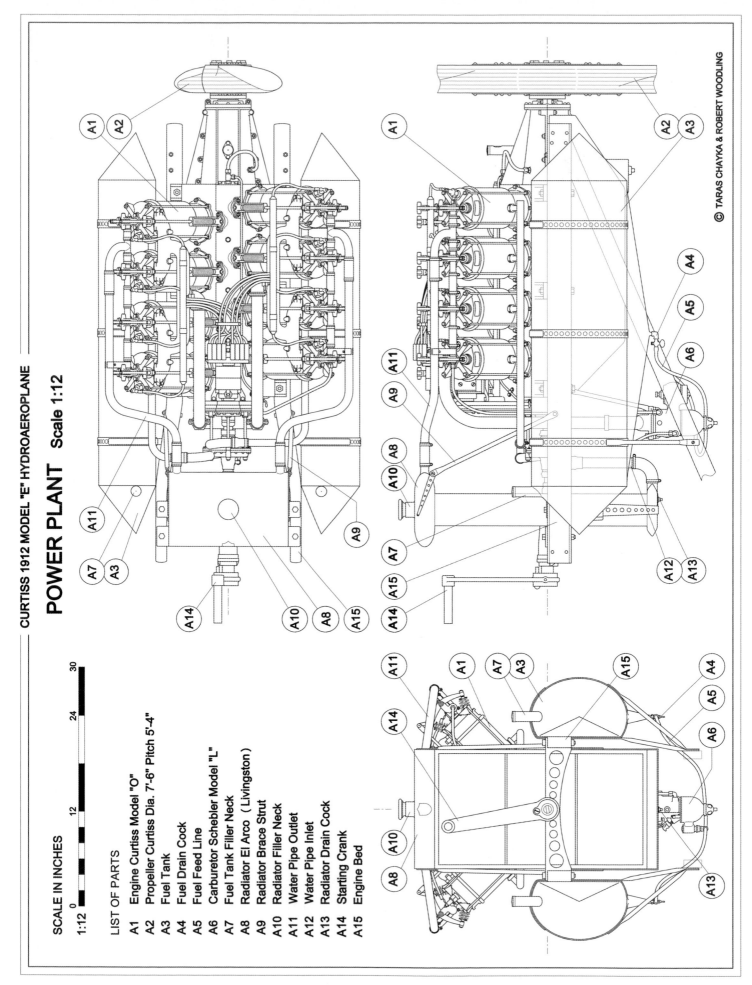

CURTISS 1912 MODEL "E" HYDROAEROPLANE

POWER PLANT   Scale 1:12

© TARAS CHAYKA & ROBERT WOODLING

SCALE IN INCHES

1:12   0   12   24   30

LIST OF PARTS

A1   Engine Curtiss Model "O"
A2   Propeller Curtiss Dia. 7'-6" Pitch 5'-4"
A3   Fuel Tank
A4   Fuel Drain Cock
A5   Fuel Feed Line
A6   Carburetor Schebler Model "L"
A7   Fuel Tank Filler Neck
A8   Radiator El Arco (Livingston)
A9   Radiator Brace Strut
A10 Radiator Filler Neck
A11 Water Pipe Outlet
A12 Water Pipe Inlet
A13 Radiator Drain Cock
A14 Starting Crank
A15 Engine Bed

CURTISS 1912 MODEL "E" HYDROAEROPLANE

POWER PLANT PARTS Scale 1:12

SCALE IN INCHES

1:12

0   12   24   30

PROPELLER

FUEL TANK

STARTING CRANK

Later version

© TARAS CHAYKA & ROBERT WOODLING

RADIATOR

ENGINE BED

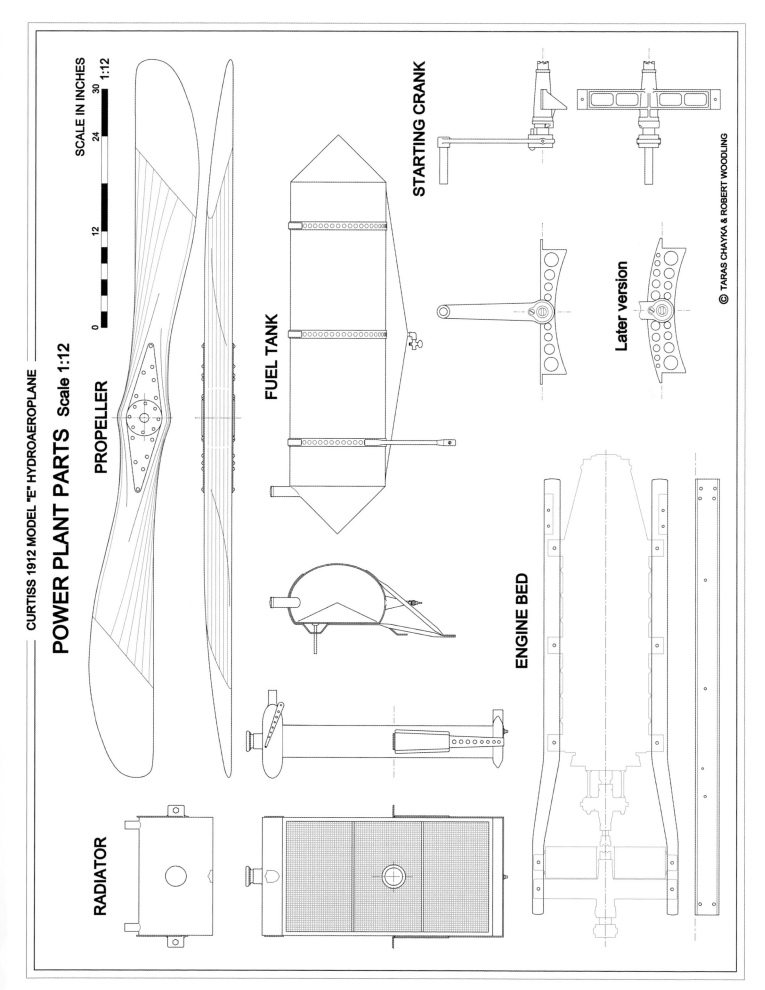

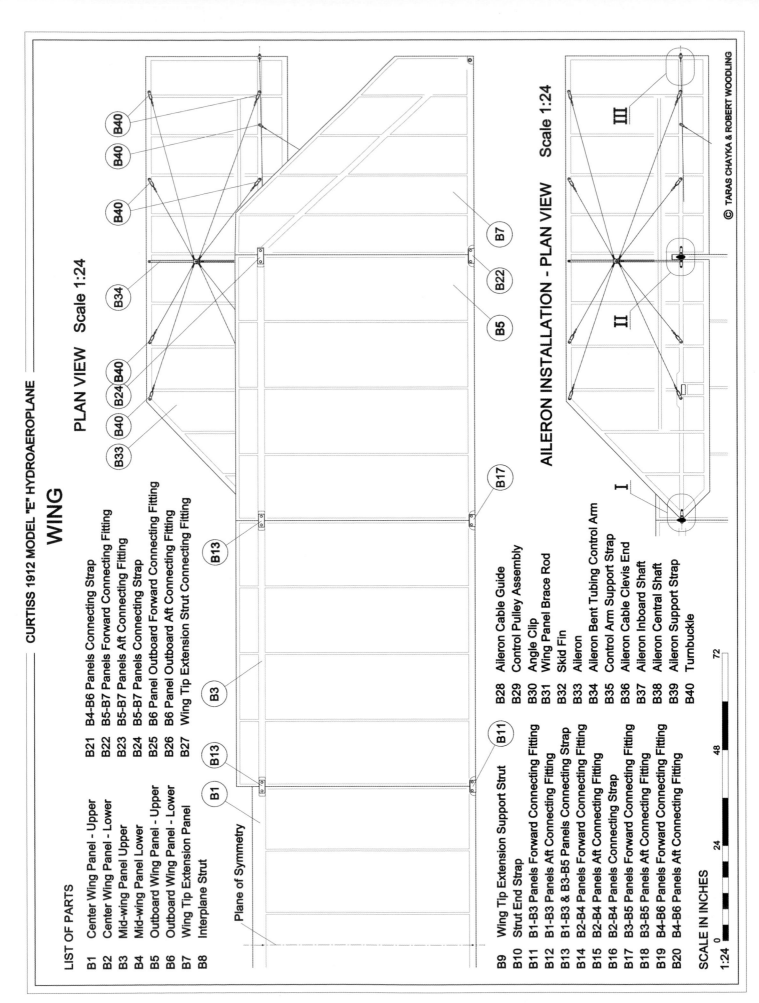

CURTISS 1912 MODEL "E" HYDROAEROPLANE

WING

PLAN VIEW   Scale 1:24

AILERON INSTALLATION - PLAN VIEW   Scale 1:24

© TARAS CHAYKA & ROBERT WOODLING

LIST OF PARTS

B1   Center Wing Panel - Upper
B2   Center Wing Panel - Lower
B3   Mid-wing Panel Upper
B4   Mid-wing Panel Lower
B5   Outboard Wing Panel - Upper
B6   Outboard Wing Panel - Lower
B7   Wing Tip Extension Panel
B8   Interplane Strut

B9   Wing Tip Extension Support Strut
B10 Strut End Strap
B11 B1-B3 Panels Forward Connecting Fitting
B12 B1-B3 Panels Aft Connecting Fitting
B13 B1-B3 & B3-B5 Panels Connecting Strap
B14 B2-B4 Panels Forward Connecting Fitting
B15 B2-B4 Panels Aft Connecting Fitting
B16 B2-B4 Panels Connecting Strap
B17 B3-B5 Panels Forward Connecting Fitting
B18 B3-B5 Panels Aft Connecting Fitting
B19 B4-B6 Panels Forward Connecting Fitting
B20 B4-B6 Panels Aft Connecting Fitting

B21 B4-B6 Panels Connecting Strap
B22 B5-B7 Panels Forward Connecting Fitting
B23 B5-B7 Panels Aft Connecting Fitting
B24 B5-B7 Panels Connecting Strap
B25 B6 Panel Outboard Forward Connecting Fitting
B26 B6 Panel Outboard Aft Connecting Fitting
B27 Wing Tip Extension Strut Connecting Fitting

B28 Aileron Cable Guide
B29 Control Pulley Assembly
B30 Angle Clip
B31 Wing Panel Brace Rod
B32 Skid Fin
B33 Aileron
B34 Aileron Bent Tubing Control Arm
B35 Control Arm Support Strap
B36 Aileron Cable Clevis End
B37 Aileron Inboard Shaft
B38 Aileron Central Shaft
B39 Aileron Support Strap
B40 Turnbuckle

Plane of Symmetry

SCALE IN INCHES

1:24   0   24   48   72

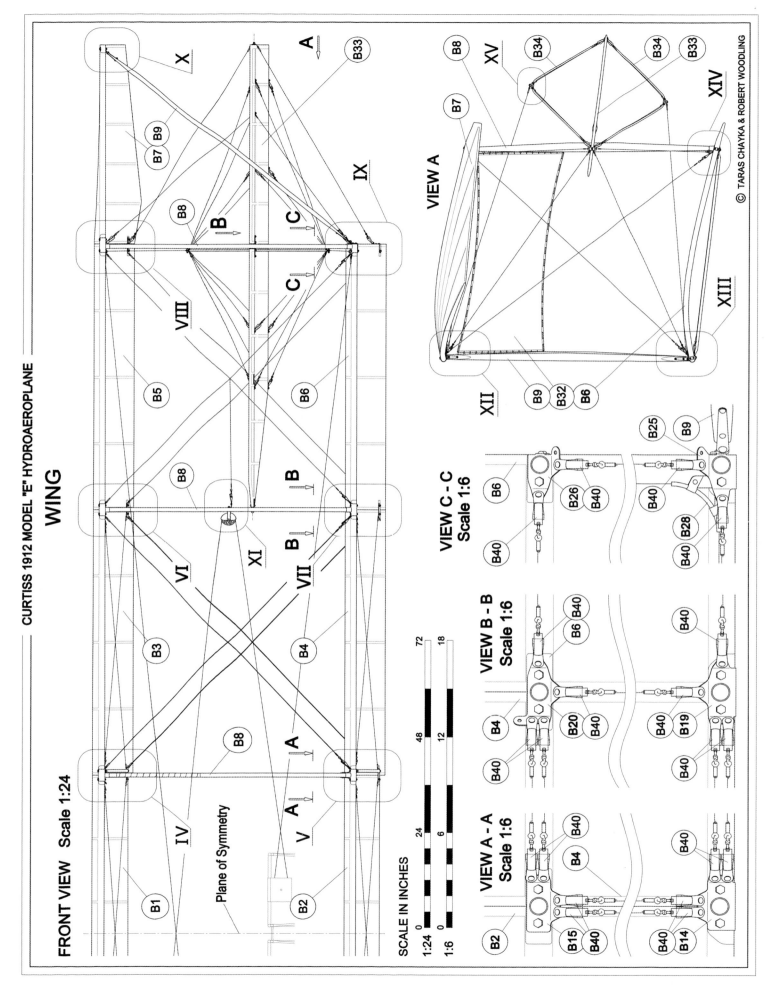

CURTISS 1912 MODEL "E" HYDROAEROPLANE

WING

FRONT VIEW Scale 1:24

Plane of Symmetry

VIEW A

VIEW C - C
Scale 1:6

VIEW B - B
Scale 1:6

VIEW A - A
Scale 1:6

SCALE IN INCHES

1:24
1:6

© TARAS CHAYKA & ROBERT WOODLING

131

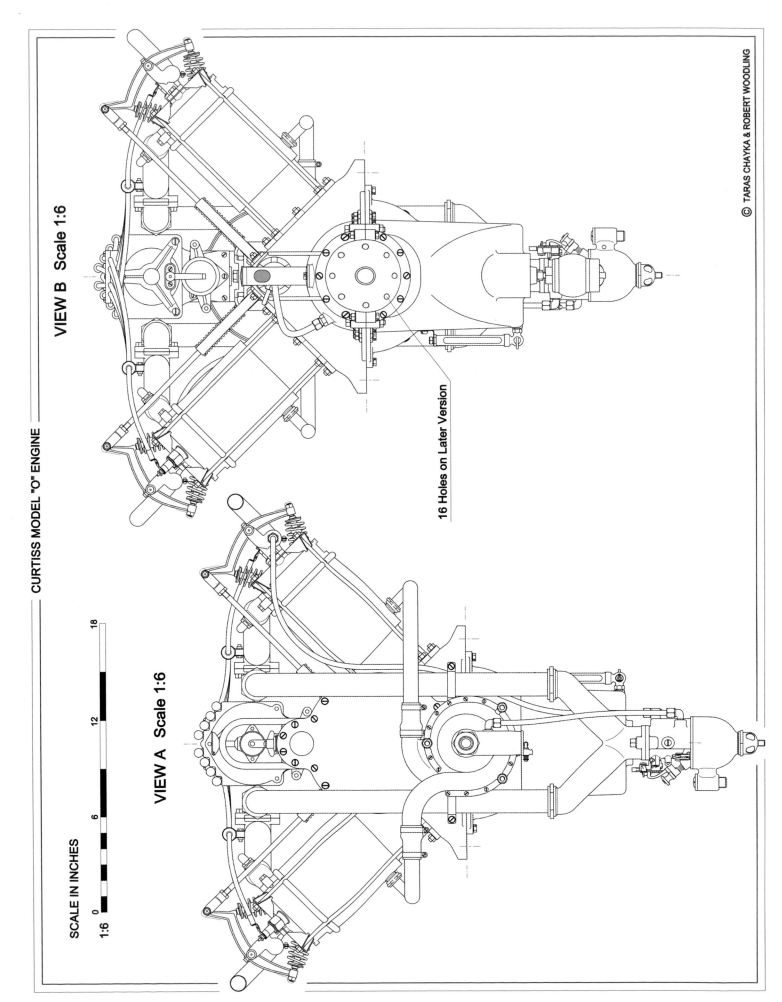

CURTISS MODEL "O" ENGINE

VIEW B Scale 1:6

16 Holes on Later Version

VIEW A Scale 1:6

SCALE IN INCHES

1:6

0   6   12   18

© TARAS CHAYKA & ROBERT WOODLING

144

LATER VERSION WITH REINFORCED CRANK CASE
AND STARTING CRANK CONNECTION (Left hand cylinder bank is not shown)
Scale 1:6

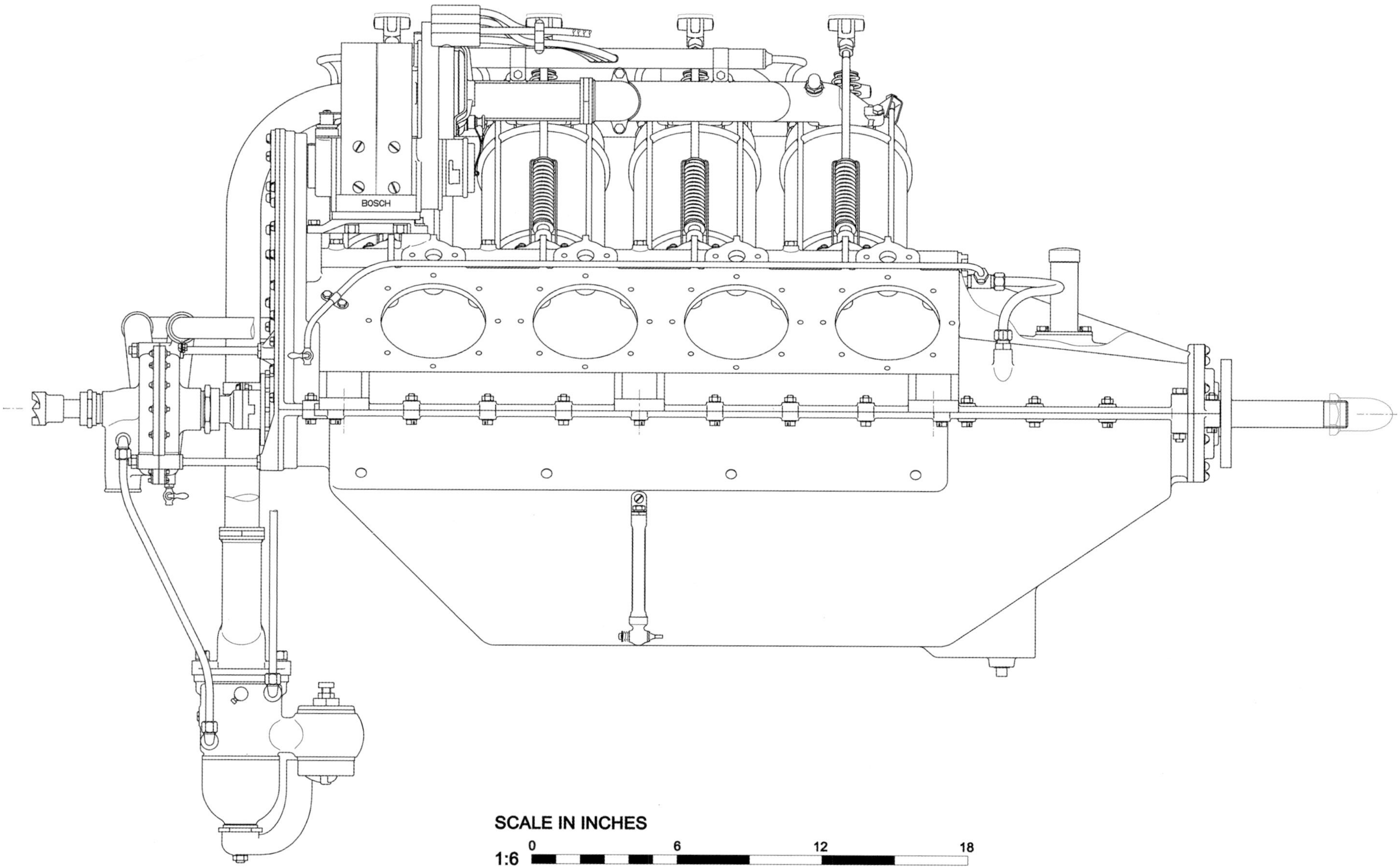

SCALE IN INCHES

1:6   0   6   12   18

© TARAS CHAYKA & ROBERT WOODLING

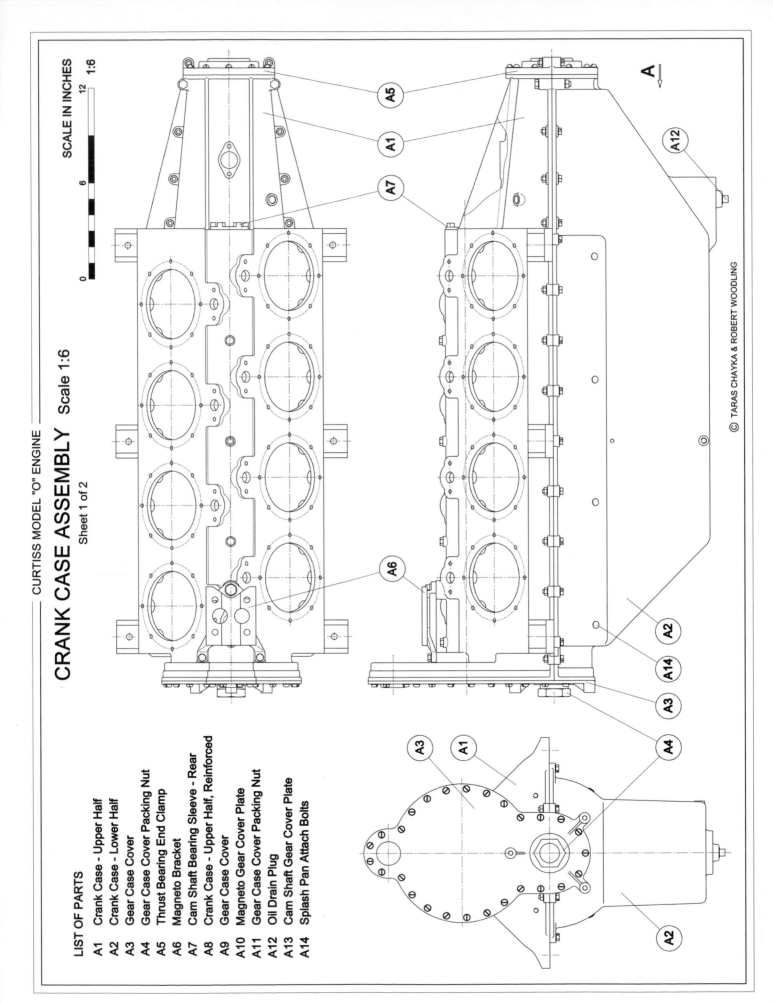

CURTISS MODEL "O" ENGINE

CRANK CASE ASSEMBLY   Scale 1:6

Sheet 1 of 2

SCALE IN INCHES

1:6

LIST OF PARTS

A1   Crank Case - Upper Half
A2   Crank Case - Lower Half
A3   Gear Case Cover
A4   Gear Case Cover Packing Nut
A5   Thrust Bearing End Clamp
A6   Magneto Bracket
A7   Cam Shaft Bearing Sleeve - Rear
A8   Crank Case - Upper Half, Reinforced
A9   Gear Case Cover
A10 Magneto Gear Cover Plate
A11 Gear Case Cover Packing Nut
A12 Oil Drain Plug
A13 Cam Shaft Gear Cover Plate
A14 Splash Pan Attach Bolts

© TARAS CHAYKA & ROBERT WOODLING

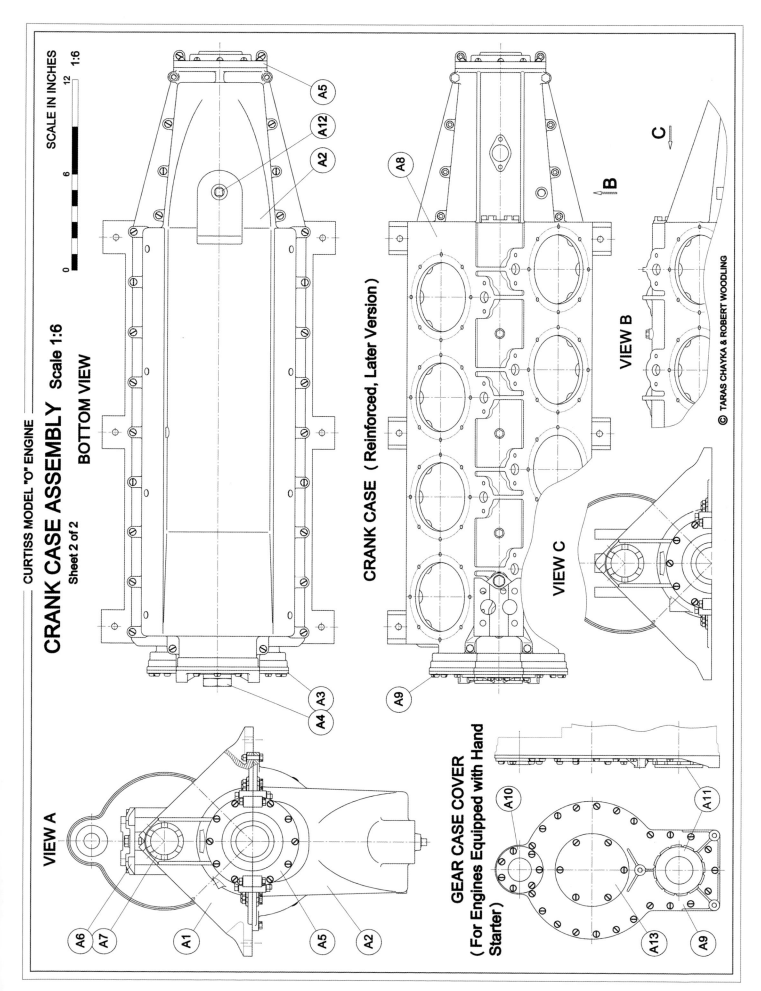

CURTISS MODEL "O" ENGINE

CRANK CASE ASSEMBLY Scale 1:6

Sheet 2 of 2

BOTTOM VIEW

SCALE IN INCHES

1:6

CRANK CASE (Reinforced, Later Version)

VIEW A

VIEW B

VIEW C

GEAR CASE COVER
(For Engines Equipped with Hand Starter)

© TARAS CHAYKA & ROBERT WOODLING

147

CURTISS MODEL "O" ENGINE

CYLINDER & VALVE GEARING SYSTEM PARTS Scale 1:4

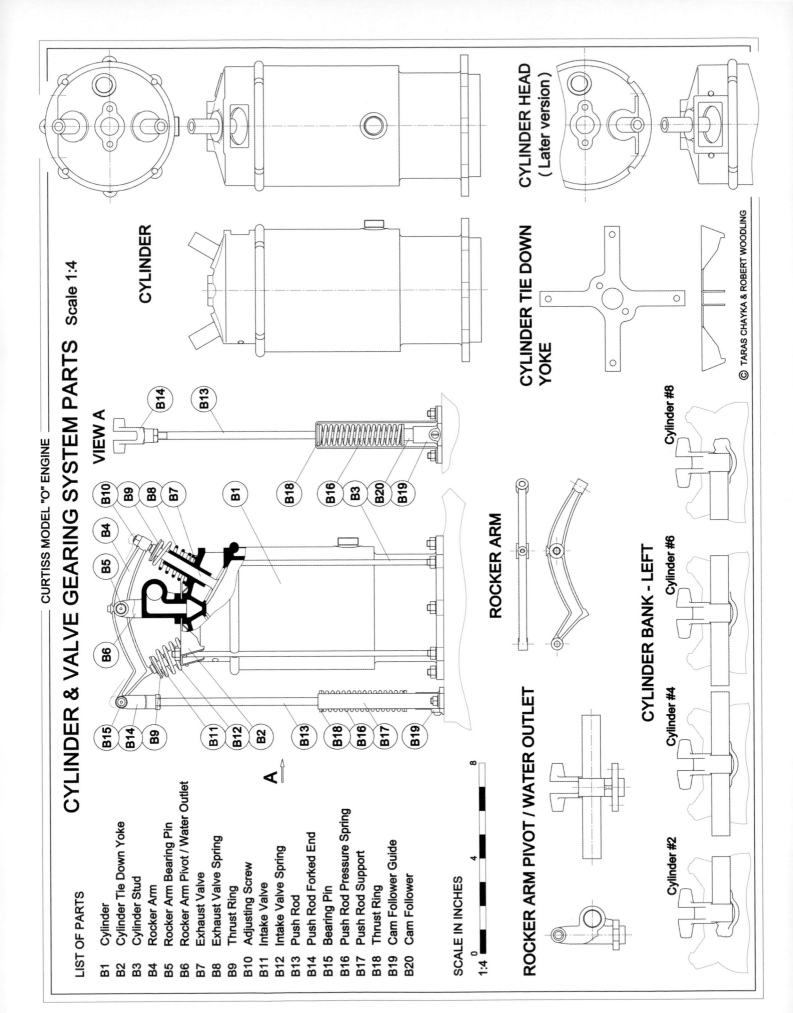

CYLINDER

CYLINDER HEAD
(Later version)

CYLINDER TIE DOWN YOKE

VIEW A

ROCKER ARM

ROCKER ARM PIVOT / WATER OUTLET

CYLINDER BANK - LEFT

Cylinder #2   Cylinder #4   Cylinder #6   Cylinder #8

LIST OF PARTS

B1   Cylinder
B2   Cylinder Tie Down Yoke
B3   Cylinder Stud
B4   Rocker Arm
B5   Rocker Arm Bearing Pin
B6   Rocker Arm Pivot / Water Outlet
B7   Exhaust Valve
B8   Exhaust Valve Spring
B9   Thrust Ring
B10 Adjusting Screw
B11 Intake Valve
B12 Intake Valve Spring
B13 Push Rod
B14 Push Rod Forked End
B15 Bearing Pin
B16 Push Rod Pressure Spring
B17 Push Rod Support
B18 Thrust Ring
B19 Cam Follower Guide
B20 Cam Follower

SCALE IN INCHES

0   4   8

1:4

© TARAS CHAYKA & ROBERT WOODLING

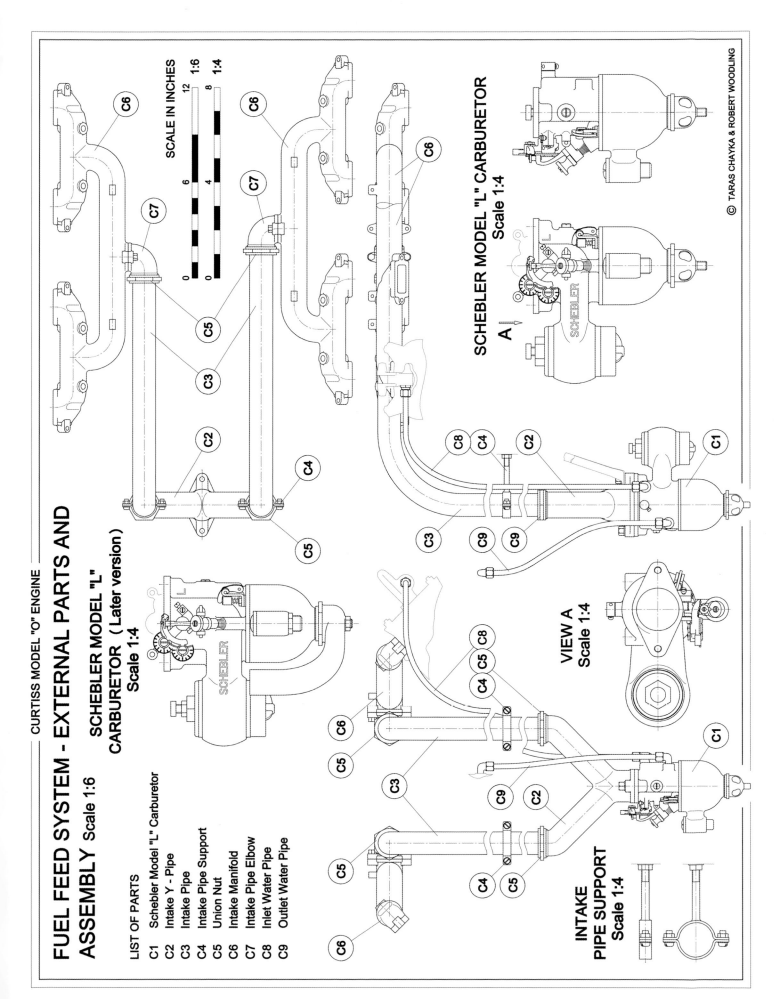

CURTISS MODEL "O" ENGINE

FUEL FEED SYSTEM - EXTERNAL PARTS AND
ASSEMBLY Scale 1:6

SCHEBLER MODEL "L"
CARBURETOR (Later version)
Scale 1:4

LIST OF PARTS

C1 Schebler Model "L" Carburetor
C2 Intake Y - Pipe
C3 Intake Pipe
C4 Intake Pipe Support
C5 Union Nut
C6 Intake Manifold
C7 Intake Pipe Elbow
C8 Inlet Water Pipe
C9 Outlet Water Pipe

SCALE IN INCHES

12   1:6
8   1:4

SCHEBLER MODEL "L" CARBURETOR
Scale 1:4

A

VIEW A
Scale 1:4

INTAKE
PIPE SUPPORT
Scale 1:4

© TARAS CHAYKA & ROBERT WOODLING

WATER COOLING SYSTEM - EXTERNAL PARTS AND ASSEMBLY   Scale 1:6

LIST OF PARTS

D1	Water Pump	D8	Water Outlet Pipe Connection
D2	Water Pump Support Stud	D9	Water Outlet Elbow Connection
D3	Water Pet Cock	D10	Water Pipe Clip
D4	Water Inlet Pipe -Left	D11	Water Pipe Clip
D5	Water Inlet Pipe - Right	D12	Water Inlet Pipe Connection
D6	Union Nut	D13	Water Pipe Clip
D7	Water Outlet Elbow	D14	Water Pipe Clip

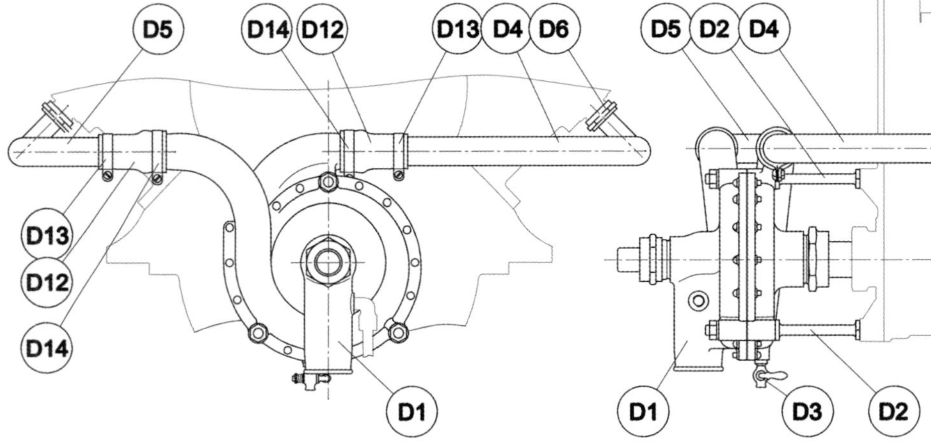

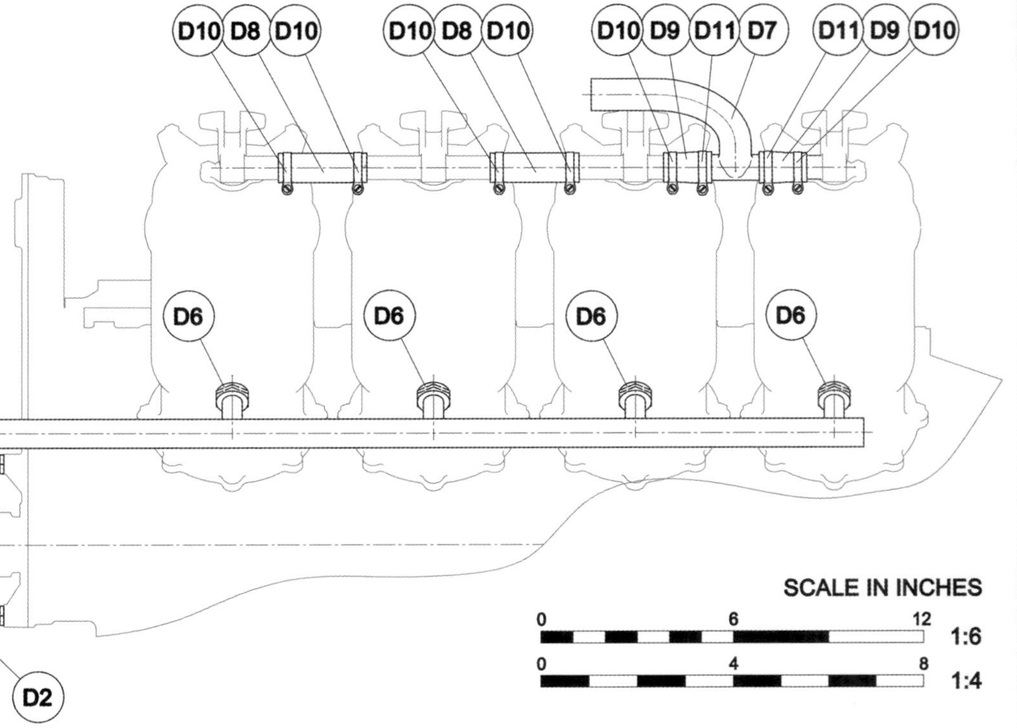

SCALE IN INCHES

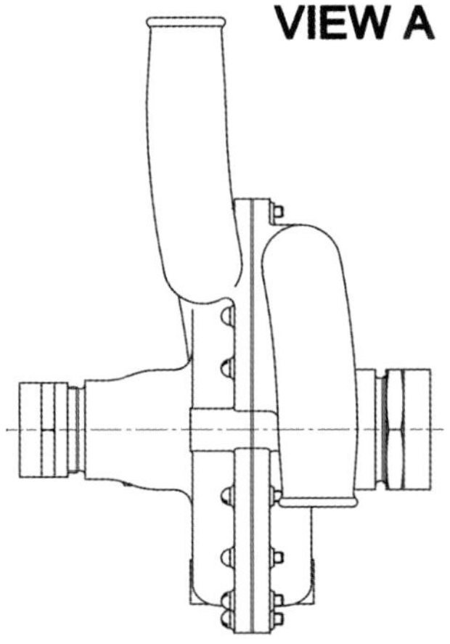

WATER PUMP CASE   Scale 1:4

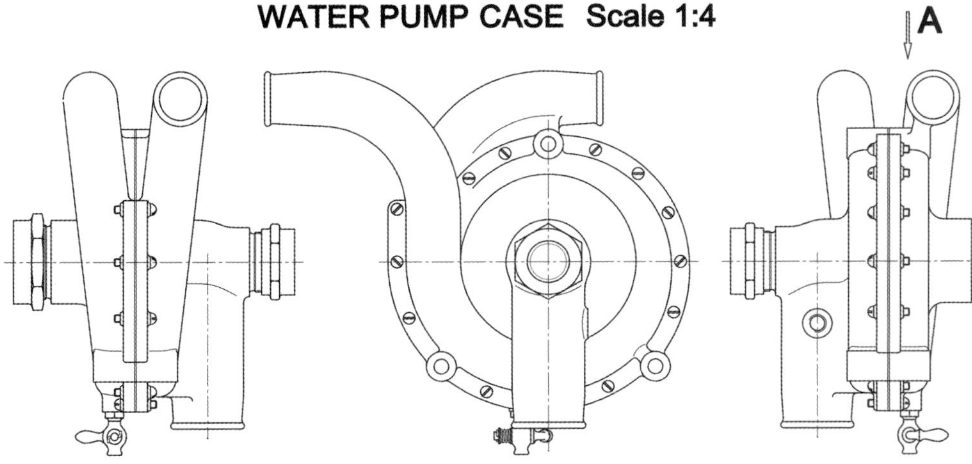

VIEW A

WATER OUTLET
ELBOW
Scale 1:4

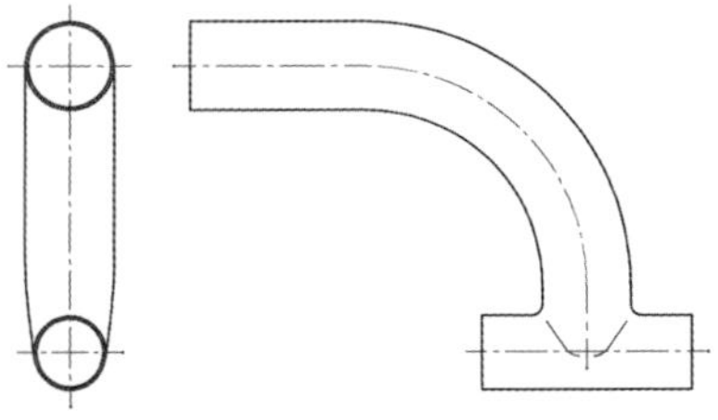

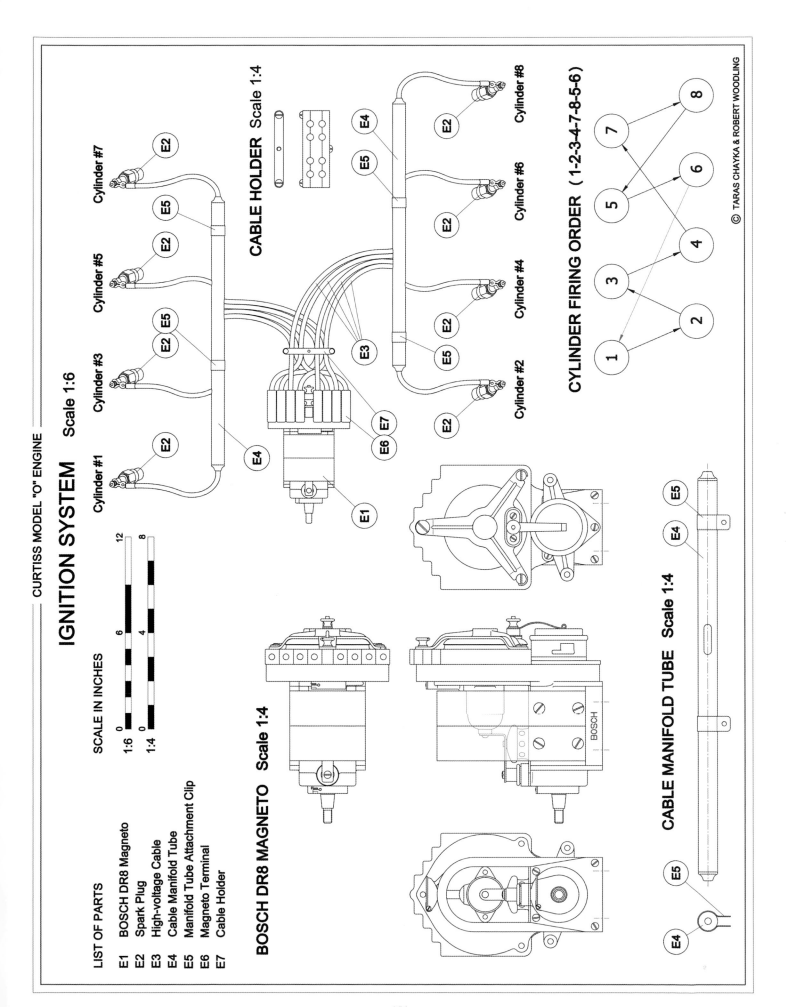

CURTISS MODEL "O" ENGINE

IGNITION SYSTEM   Scale 1:6

LIST OF PARTS

E1 BOSCH DR8 Magneto
E2 Spark Plug
E3 High-voltage Cable
E4 Cable Manifold Tube
E5 Manifold Tube Attachment Clip
E6 Magneto Terminal
E7 Cable Holder

SCALE IN INCHES

CABLE HOLDER   Scale 1:4

BOSCH DR8 MAGNETO   Scale 1:4

CABLE MANIFOLD TUBE   Scale 1:4

CYLINDER FIRING ORDER (1-2-3-4-7-8-5-6)

Cylinder #1 Cylinder #3 Cylinder #5 Cylinder #7

Cylinder #2 Cylinder #4 Cylinder #6 Cylinder #8

© TARAS CHAYKA & ROBERT WOODLING

151

OIL SYSTEM - EXTERNAL PARTS AND ASSEMBLY Scale 1:6

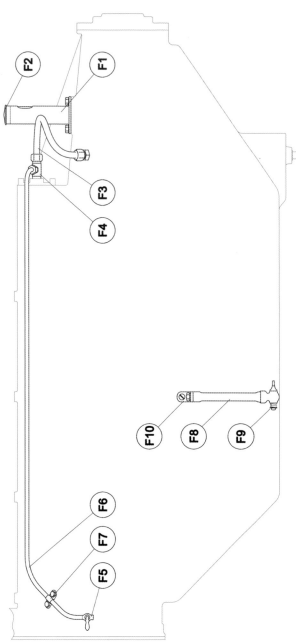

LIST OF PARTS

F1   Oil Filler Pipe
F2   Oil Filler Cap
F3   Oil Inlet Pipe
F4   Tee
F5   Oil Bleeder Pet Cock
F6   Oil Bleeder Pipe
F7   Oil Bleeder Pipe Clip
F8   Oil Sight Glass
F9   Oil Bleeder Pet Cock
F10 Oil Sight Glass Bracket

OIL SIGHT GLASS
Scale 1:2

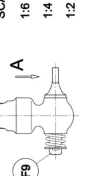
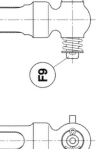
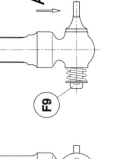

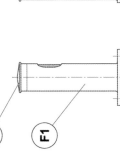
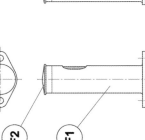

OIL FILLER PIPE
(Later version)
Scale 1:4

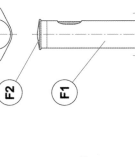

OIL FILLER PIPE
Scale 1:4

OIL BLEEDER PET COCK
Scale 1:2

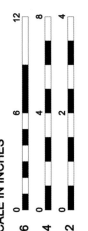
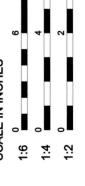

VIEW A

SCALE IN INCHES

1:6
1:4
1:2

© TARAS CHAYKA & ROBERT WOODLING

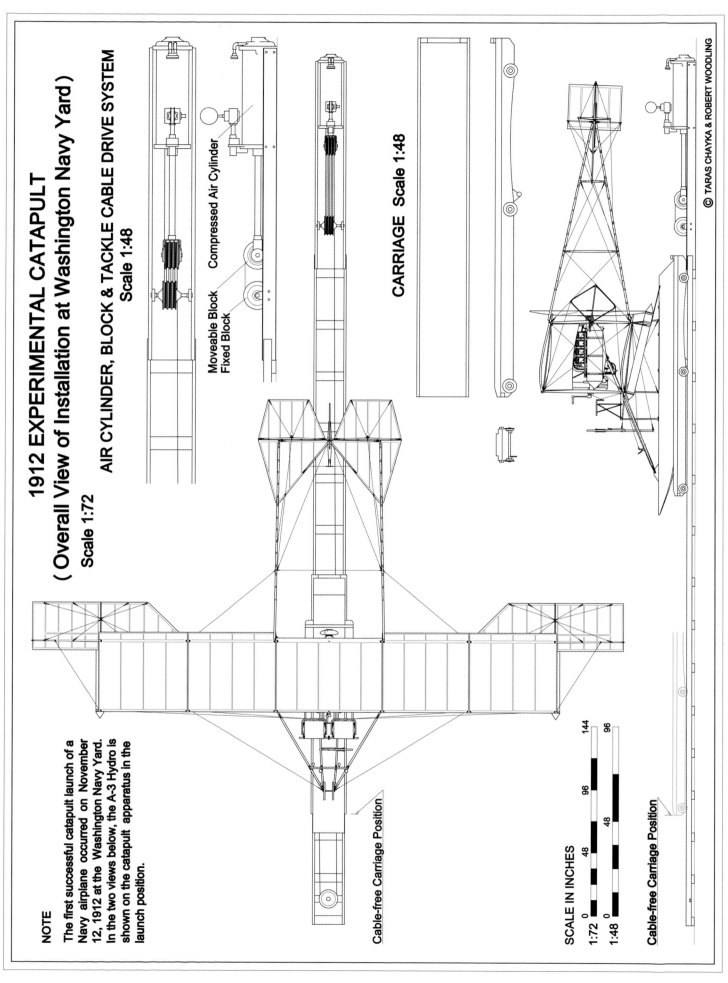

1912 EXPERIMENTAL CATAPULT
(Overall View of Installation at Washington Navy Yard)
Scale 1:72

AIR CYLINDER, BLOCK & TACKLE CABLE DRIVE SYSTEM
Scale 1:48

Compressed Air Cylinder

Moveable Block
Fixed Block

CARRIAGE Scale 1:48

© TARAS CHAYKA & ROBERT WOODLING

NOTE

The first successful catapult launch of a
Navy airplane occurred on November
12, 1912 at the Washington Navy Yard.
In the two views below, the A-3 Hydro is
shown on the catapult apparatus in the
launch position.

Cable-free Carriage Position

SCALE IN INCHES

1:72   0   48   96   144

1:48   0   48   96

Cable-free Carriage Position

153

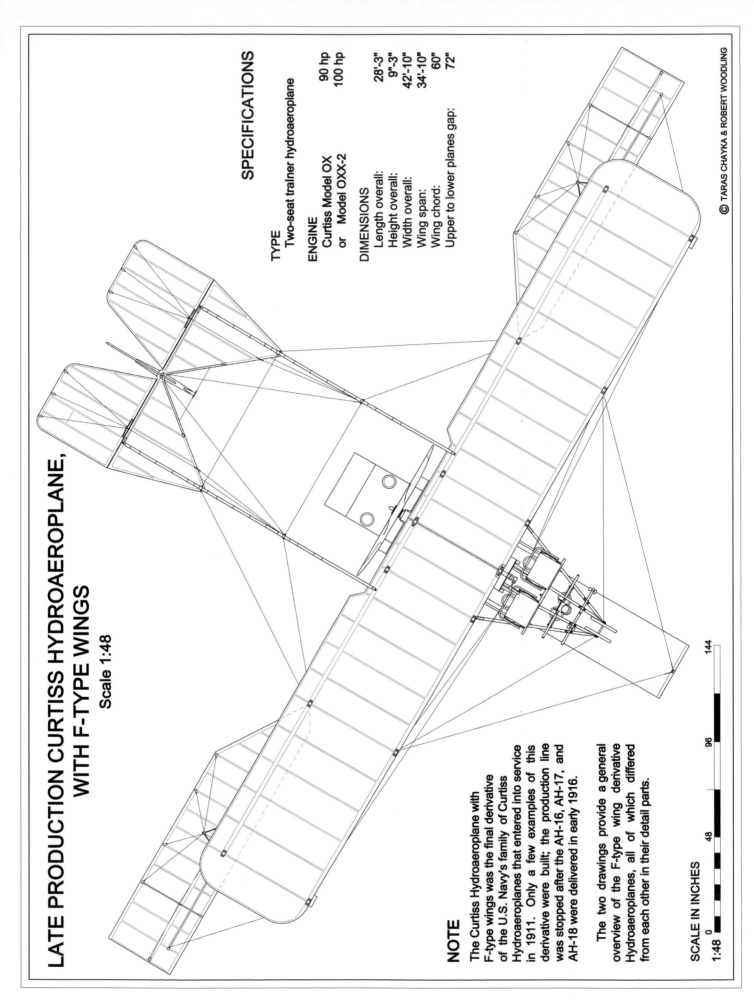

LATE PRODUCTION CURTISS HYDROAEROPLANE, WITH F-TYPE WINGS

Scale 1:48

SPECIFICATIONS

TYPE
Two-seat trainer hydroaeroplane

ENGINE
Curtiss Model OX   90 hp
or   Model OXX-2   100 hp

DIMENSIONS
Length overall: 28'-3"
Height overall: 9"-3"
Width overall: 42'-10"
Wing span: 34'-10"
Wing chord: 60"
Upper to lower planes gap: 72"

© TARAS CHAYKA & ROBERT WOODLING

NOTE

The Curtiss Hydroaeroplane with F-type wings was the final derivative of the U.S. Navy's family of Curtiss Hydroaeroplanes that entered into service in 1911. Only a few examples of this derivative were built; the production line was stopped after the AH-16, AH-17, and AH-18 were delivered in early 1916.

The two drawings provide a general overview of the F-type wing derivative Hydroaeroplanes, all of which differed from each other in their detail parts.

SCALE IN INCHES

0   48   96   144

1:48

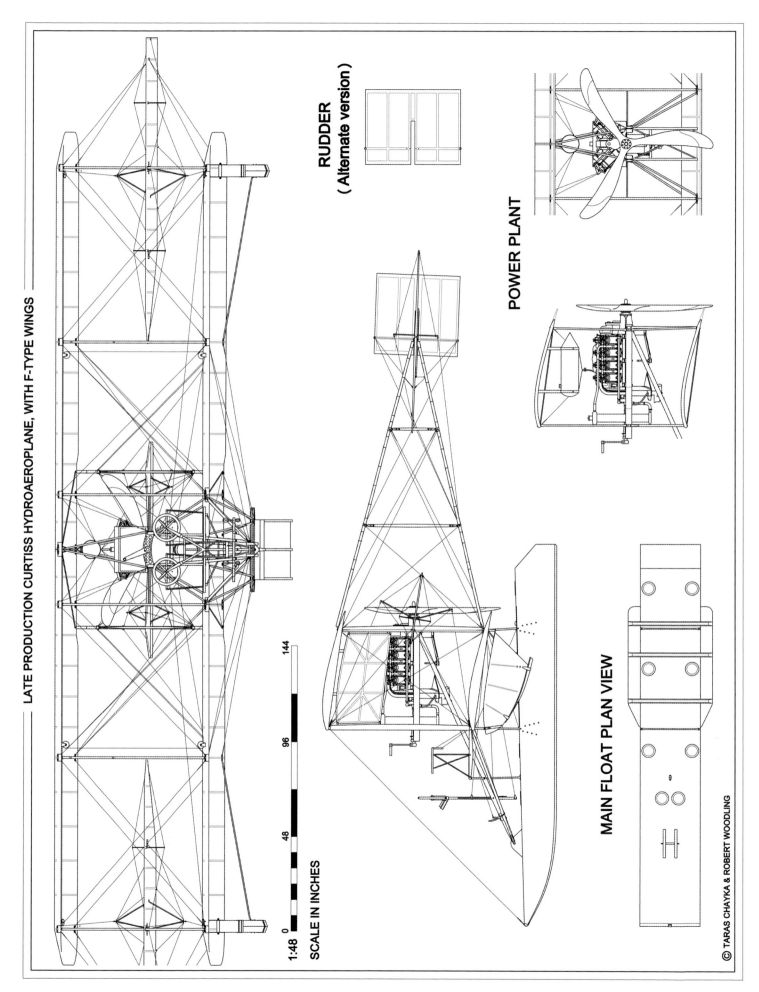

LATE PRODUCTION CURTISS HYDROAEROPLANE, WITH F-TYPE WINGS

RUDDER
(Alternate version)

POWER PLANT

MAIN FLOAT PLAN VIEW

SCALE IN INCHES

1:48   0   48   96   144

© TARAS CHAYKA & ROBERT WOODLING

155

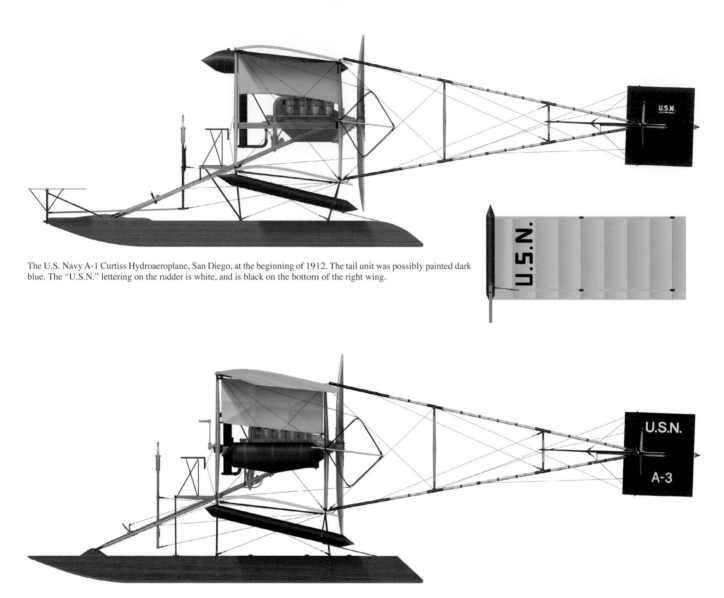

The U.S. Navy A-1 Curtiss Hydroaeroplane, San Diego, at the beginning of 1912. The tail unit was possibly painted dark blue. The "U.S.N." lettering on the rudder is white, and is black on the bottom of the right wing.

The U.S. Navy A-3 Curtiss Hydroaeroplane, Guantanamo Bay, early 1913. The tail unit was also possibly painted dark blue. The "U.S.N." and "A-3" lettering on the rudder is white.

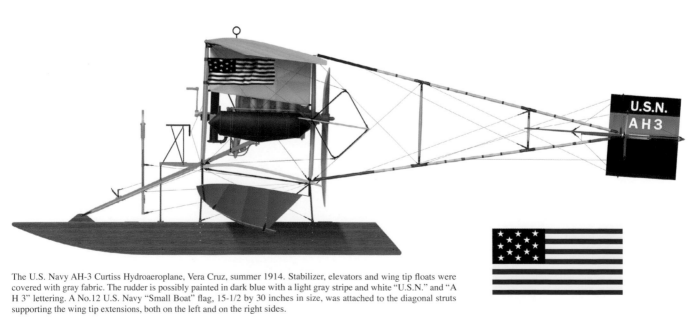

The U.S. Navy AH-3 Curtiss Hydroaeroplane, Vera Cruz, summer 1914. Stabilizer, elevators and wing tip floats were covered with gray fabric. The rudder is possibly painted in dark blue with a light gray stripe and white "U.S.N." and "A H 3" lettering. A No.12 U.S. Navy "Small Boat" flag, 15-1/2 by 30 inches in size, was attached to the diagonal struts supporting the wing tip extensions, both on the left and on the right sides.

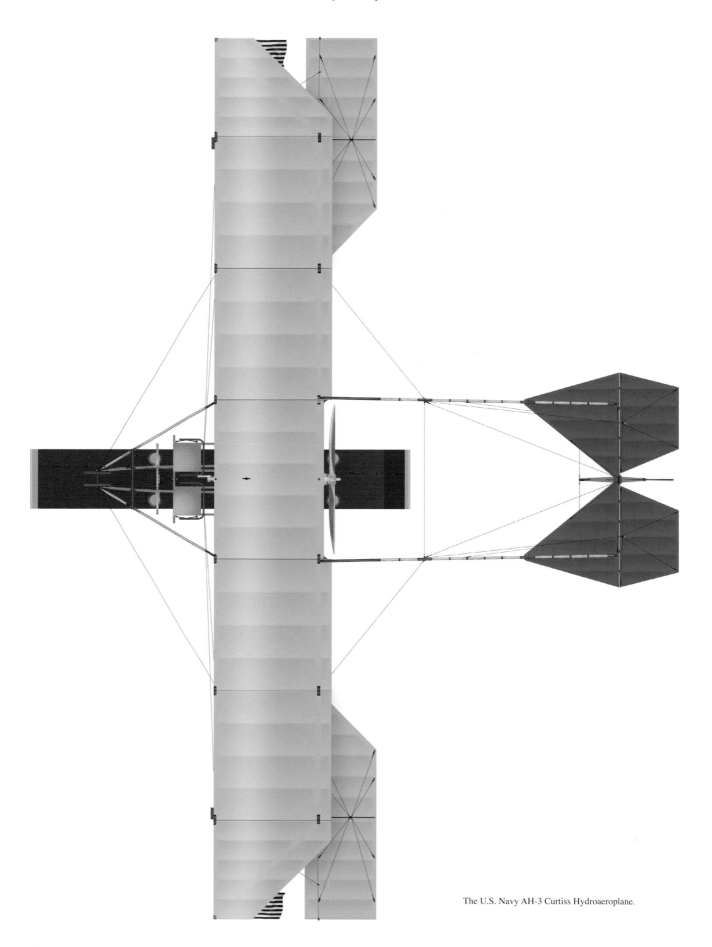

The U.S. Navy AH-3 Curtiss Hydroaeroplane.

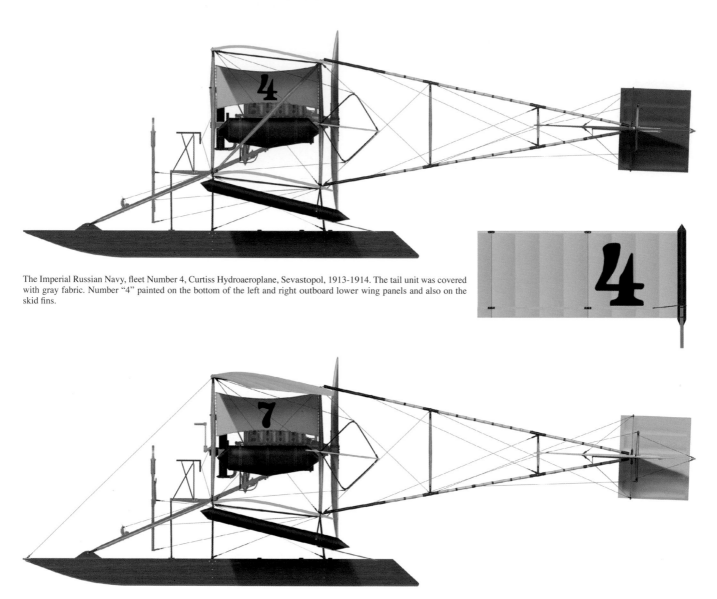

The Imperial Russian Navy, fleet Number 4, Curtiss Hydroaeroplane, Sevastopol, 1913-1914. The tail unit was covered with gray fabric. Number "4" painted on the bottom of the left and right outboard lower wing panels and also on the skid fins.

The Imperial Russian Navy, fleet Number 7, Curtiss Hydroaeroplane, Sevastopol, 1913-1914. Black number "7" painted only on the skid fins.

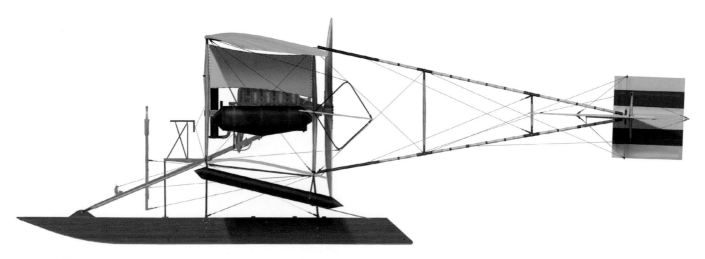

The Imperial Japanese Navy Yokosho Type Ka seaplane, c.1912-1913. Overall in light colored fabric, with two wide red or black stripes painted on the rudder.

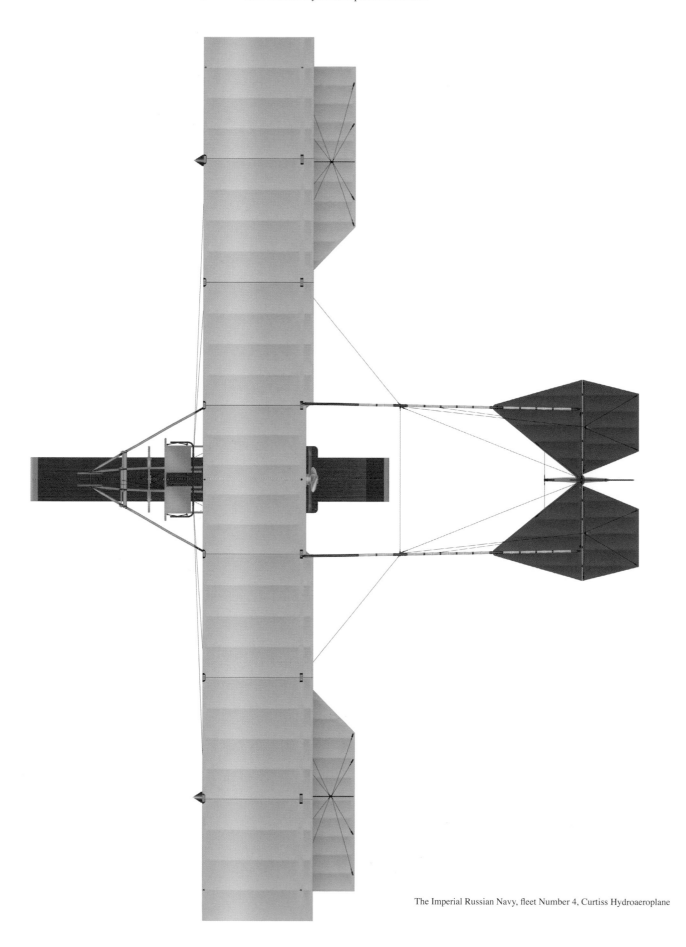

The Imperial Russian Navy, fleet Number 4, Curtiss Hydroaeroplane

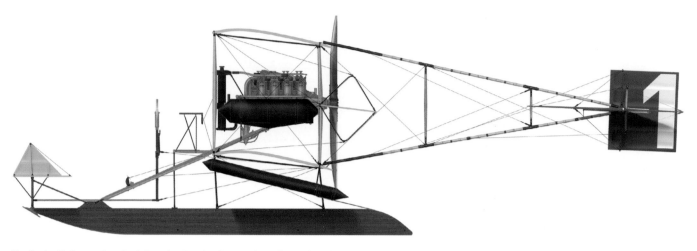

The Curtiss Hydroaeroplane that belonged to French aviator Louis Paulhan. With this machine Paulhan took part in a seaplane competition at Monaco in 1912. The fuel tank was fitted only on the left side; only one pilot seat was installed in place of two. The tail unit was covered with gray fabric. White race number "1" was painted on both sides of the rudder.

Curtiss model E Hydroaeroplane used by Al Engel, one of the American pioneers of aviation. Northeastern Ohio, c.1913-1914. The Lakewood Yacht Club burgee in blue and red is on the rudder. Black lettering "Al. J. Engel" on the skid fins.

The same Hydro during summer 1914. The name of the airplane, "Bumble Bee" was painted in black on the rudder. Inscriptions on the skid fins: "Al. J. Engel", "U.S. Air Mail" and "Route No.* - A - 607004" are also in black. The "Bee" emblems were placed on the upper wing tip extensions, in four positions. A warning note, "Do not step on the float" was painted in yellow on the upper nose part of the float.

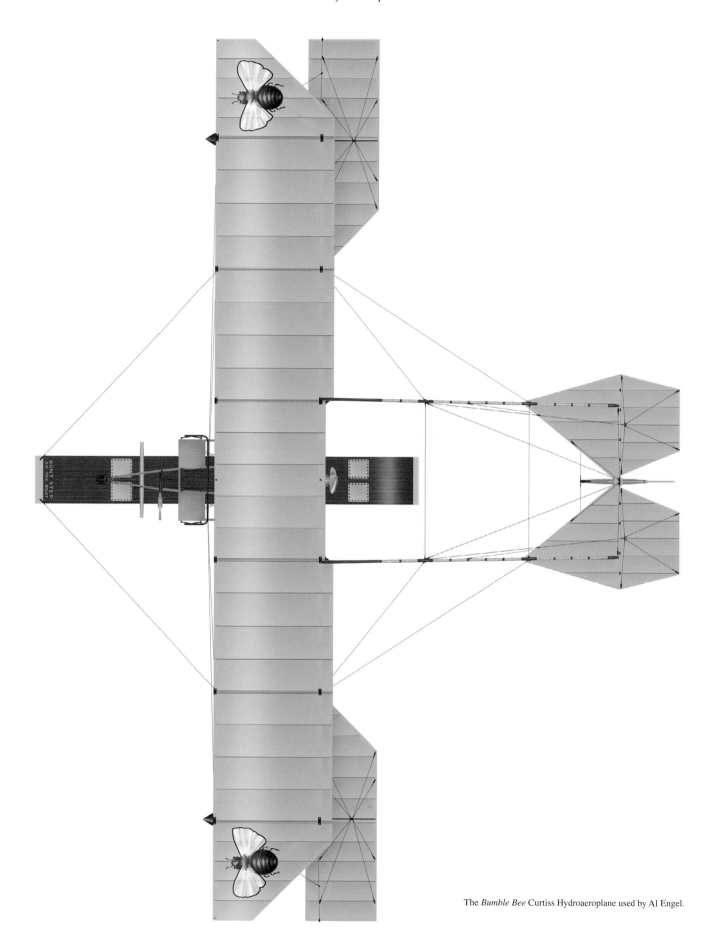

The *Bumble Bee* Curtiss Hydroaeroplane used by Al Engel.

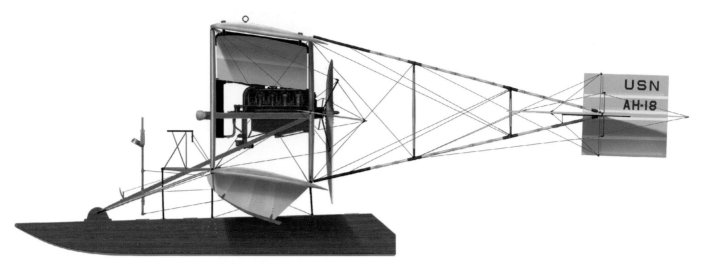

The U.S. Navy late production AH-18, an F-winged Curtiss Hydroaeroplane, Pensacola, 1916. This airplane had no insignia other than the black "USN AH-18" lettering on the rudder.

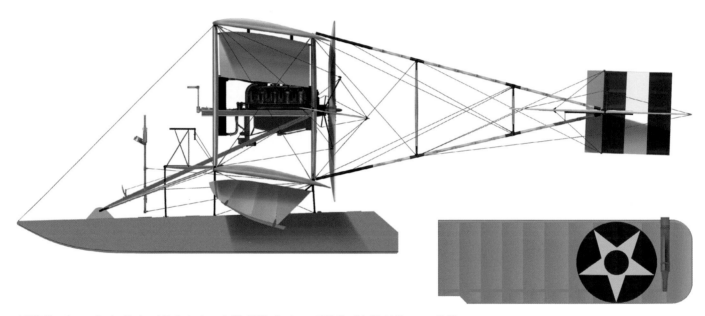

A U.S. Navy late production F-winged Hydro in the early World War I colors, c.1917. English Khaki Gray overall. The "star in circle" insignia was painted backwards on the wings, in four positions. Three-color, red, white and blue stripes are on the rudder.

CHAPTER 7

Curtiss Hydroaeroplanes and Replicas in Museums

Several replicas and one authentic Curtiss Hydroaeroplane are now on display in museums in the United States and in Italy. Some of these aircraft have flown at least one time, while some of them are non-flying full-scale models. Each of these Curtiss Hydros has become one of the most interesting exhibits in the museums, drawing the attention of visitors with its unique combination of biplane wings, pontoon, pusher propeller, and exposed pilot.

Glenn H. Curtiss Museum, Hammondsport, New York

Incorporated in 1961, the Curtiss Museum is dedicated to bringing before the public the accomplishments of early motorcycle manufacturer and aviation pioneer Glenn Hammond Curtiss. The museum is located just outside Hammondsport, a small town on the shore of Lake Keuka, in a historical place, where Glenn Curtiss's factory, airplane test facility and pilot training school were located during the beginning of the last century. And between 1911 and 1916, here is where the Hydros were

Curtiss Hydroaeroplane flying replica in the exhibition hall of the Glenn H. Curtiss Museum, at Hammondsport, NY. *Taras Chayka Photo Collection.*

designed, built and tested. The museum houses a priceless collection of historic aircraft, motorcycles, and other artifacts of Curtiss origin. In addition to seeing the museum displays and exhibits, visitors are welcome to enter the Restoration Shop, talk with volunteer craftsmen, and watch them as they work on the restoration of historic aircraft.

Completed by the Museum's restoration shop in 2004, the replica A-1 has performed beautifully in flights during September's Seaplane Homecomings of 2004, 2005 and 2006 at Hammondsport. Piloted by Jim Poel, the A-1 demonstrated several firsts in 2005. It was flown with a new float, new wheels and anti-skid panels. It was flown higher and faster, and made its first turn and taxied with two persons on board. In 2006, Poel flew the A-1 to the Bluff and back – a distance of 7 miles. Also achieved in 2006 was a flight with 2 persons aboard and a full tank of gas. This airplane is equipped with a Curtiss OX-5 engine and interestingly today it is the only flying replica of a Curtiss Hydroaeroplane on which the original control system (the roll control is carried out by the pilot leaning his body from side to side) has been reproduced.

National Naval Aviation Museum, Pensacola, Florida
In commemoration of the fiftieth anniversary of U.S. naval aviation in 1961, the Navy joined with the Institute of Aerospace Sciences in San Diego to construct two exact replicas of the Curtiss A-1 *Triad*, which was the first aircraft procured by the U.S. Navy. The work of some 130 volunteers and a few employees of the Overhaul and Repair Department on board Naval Air Station (NAS) North Island, California, came to fruition in July 1961, when one of the *Triads* actually took flight over San Diego Bay. Piloted by Naval Reserve Commander Don Germeraad, Chief Engineering Test Pilot for the Convair Division of General Dynamics, the replica A-1 made multiple flights reaching an altitude of 100 ft. on one of them. "Now I know how the other

The A-1 static display replica being unloaded from a USMC Lockheed GV-1 at Anacostia Naval Air Station, Oct. 1961. *U.S. Naval History and Heritage Command Photograph.*

And today this replica of the A-1 is being exhibited in the National Museum of Naval Aviation at Pensacola. *Taras Chayka Photo Collection.*

half lived – the half century of pilots, that is," Germeraad commented after the flight. "My hat is off to the old-timers. It is really amazing what they accomplished with what they had to work with."

In addition to the flying replica, which was modified to include a more powerful horsepower engine, metal in place of bamboo in the tail boom, and laminated ash instead of spruce for spars, the Navy/IAS team also constructed a replica A-1 that was not intended to fly. Following the commemoration events in San Diego, it was donated to the Smithsonian National Air Museum (now National Air and Space Museum) while the flying replica remained in California for display in the San Diego Aerospace Museum. It was lost in a fire at the museum in 1978.

The Smithsonian's A-1 first arrived at NAS Pensacola, Florida, for display at the Naval Aviation Museum (now National Museum of Naval Aviation) in 1968. It remained on loan until 1992, at which time custody was transferred to the museum. This replica is equipped with the only surviving example of the original Curtiss Model O engine.

San Diego Air and Space Museum, San Diego, California
An affiliate of the Smithsonian Institution, the Museum houses a collection of historic aircraft and spacecraft from all over the world, including a working flying replica of Lindbergh's Spirit of St. Louis, the actual Apollo 9 Command Module spacecraft and the only real GPS satellite on display in the world.

Suspended from the ceiling in the rotunda is a reproduction of a Curtiss A-1 *Triad*. The plane was built by Henry L. Wheeler of Rancho Bernardo and a team of Aerospace Museum volunteers, and took three years to complete. It is powered by a 90-hp Curtiss OX-5 V-8 water-cooled engine.

The Museum's Curtiss A-1 replica, registered N45644, made a total of 7 flights from the waters of San Diego Bay: two flights on January 12, three flights on January 21 and two flights on January 26, 1984. The FAA restricted the flights to a relative

After it made seven flights in 1984, this newly built A-1 replica took its place in the rotunda of the San Diego Air & Space Museum. *Robert Woodling Photo Collection.*

straight line at an altitude of less than 100 ft. near Harbor Island. The first two flights on January 12 were about 1/2 mile long and less than 100 ft. high. The next five flights, January 21 and 26 were all over a mile long and less than 100 ft. high. The seven flights were made without the wheels installed and with an original Curtiss OX5 engine.

After the flights the replica became the property of the San Diego Aerospace Museum. It was installed in its place of honor in the rotunda of the new Aerospace Museum that is housed in the former Ford Building from the park's 1935 California Pacific International Exposition. The museum's A-1 replica replaces an earlier example that was lost in a 1978 fire that destroyed the museum at its original home in Balboa Park's former Electric Building.

The Crawford Auto Aviation Museum, Cleveland, Ohio.

The Crawford Museum is a collection of the Western Reserve Historical Society, which presents the history of land and air transportation by using interesting, engaging and entertaining exhibits, displays and activities.

The Museum's hydroaeroplane was originally purchased by Clevelander Al Engel, a former member of the Curtiss Exhibition Team. Having survived a crash in his Curtiss landplane, Engel opted for a Curtiss Hydroaeroplane so he could land on water. He named his plane the *Bumble Bee*. Later, he modified it with wing tip extensions and a more powerful Curtiss "Odd-O" engine so that a friend or paying customer could ride along on a flight over Lake Erie. Al flew the Bumble Bee extensively throughout Northeastern Ohio, and for a time, based the *Bumble Bee* at the Lakewood Yacht Club (now Cuyahoga Yacht Club) at the mouth of the Rocky River. During the summer months of 1914, Al used the *Bumble Bee* to deliver "aerial mail," consisting primarily of post cards, at Lake Chautauqua, New York. Al retired the *Bumble Bee* at the end of the 1914 season, stored the plane in his garage in Cleveland, and in 1946 sold it to the Thompson Products Museum in Cleveland.

The *Bumble Bee* was restored at that time, and is now the sole remaining genuine Curtiss Hydro in the world. All of the restoration and assembly was carried out under the supervision of Al Angel. The plane has remained in very good condition. The only original detail that required replacement was a pair of turnbuckles. All other parts, except those made of fabric, are original. The wing panels, ailerons and tail unit were re-covered and coated with lacquer vanish.

Museo Storico Navale di Venezia – Naval Historical Museum of Venice, Italy
Founded in 1919 after World War I, the main museum is located in Campo San Biagio, close to the famous Venice Arsenale, in a historic 15th century building that was used for centuries as a granary. The grain was used to bake a special type of long-life bread called a "biscuit" that was suitable for use on the Venetian sailing ships that were leaving port.

A replica Curtiss Hydroaeroplane has been placed in a separate museum building and can only be viewed by prior arrangement with the military commander of the Italian Navy section of the Arsenale. The replica was originally on display at the Italian Air Force Museum (Museo Storico dell' Aeronautica Militare Italiana) at Vigna di Valle, outside Rome. In the early-1970s there was an agreement between the Italian Air Force and the Italian Navy to build two sets of replicas of early airplanes. The IAF built two single seat Curtiss Hydros, but the Navy did not complete its airplanes, so the Curtiss Hydro replicas were then kept at Vigna di Valle. One replica remained in the museum, while the other was used for temporary exhibitions until it was too worn out; then it was kept dismantled in storage. Several years ago the Italian Air Force swapped the Hydro that was in better shape with the Navy, obtaining in exchange an original Austrian engine, now installed on the Lohner flying boat in the IAF museum.

Lone Star Flight Museum, Galveston, Texas
Located at the International Airport at Scholes Field in Galveston, Texas, the museum is recognized by the State of Texas as the Texas Aviation Hall of Fame. The Museum places special educational significance on the technological evolution of American aviation and related technologies, and the impact of these developments on the progress of aviation and world events.

The museum's Curtiss Hydro is a non-flying replica built by Jim Harris and is displayed hanging from the ceiling of the museum.

Al Engel's Curtiss Hydro, *Bumble Bee*, is the only surviving original airplane of its type in the world. Now it is on display at the Crawford Auto Aviation Museum, in Cleveland, Ohio. *Taras Chayka Photo Collection*.

In the beginning of the last century Curtiss Hydroaeroplanes were also delivered to the Italian Navy. This non-flying replica of a single seat Hydro has now been placed in the Naval Historical Museum in Venice, Italy. *Taras Chayka Photo Collection.*

Curtiss Hydroaeroplane Projects in Work

The Paxtuxent River T&E Museum will be the home of a new Hydro replica that is being built by the members of EAA Chapter 478, based in Lexington Park, MD. The chapter's airplane will be a non-flying replica; it is targeted for completion in 2011.

Bibliography

Aleksandrov, Andrei O. *Amerikanskie gidroplany v Rossii, 1912-1917*. Sankt-Peterburg: [s.n.], 1999.

Alexandrov, Andrei O.,"Russian Curtisses - Curtiss Float-planes of the Imperial Russian Navy 1912 – 1915." Edited by August G. Blume. Pts. 1 and 2. *WW1 Aero: The Journal of the Early Aeroplane*, no. 164 (May 1999): 17-30; no. 165 (August 1999): 12-28.

Angle, Glenn Dale. *Airplane Engine Encyclopedia; An Alphabetically Arranged Compilation of All Available Data on the World's Airplane Engines*. Dayton, O.: The Otterbein press, 1921.

Artemyev, A. M. *Morskaya aviatsiya Rossii*. Moscow: Voyennoye Izdatelstvo, 1996.

Bignozzi, Giorgio, and B. Catalanotto. *Storia degli aerei d'Italia*. Roma: Editrice Cielo, 1962.

Bowers, Peter M. *Curtiss Aircraft, 1907-1947*. London: Putnam, 1979.

Brockett, Paul. *Bibliography of Aeronautics 1909-1916*. Washington: US G.P.O., 1921.

Carpenter, Jack. *Pendulum II: The Story of America's Three Aviation Pioneers, Wilbur Wright, Orville Wright, and Glenn Curtiss, the "Henry Ford of Aviation" : Including How the Partnership of Alexander Graham Bell and Glenn Hammond Curtiss Led to the Founding of the American Aviation Industry*. San Juan Capistrano, CA: Arsdalen, Bosch & Co, 2003.

Casey Louis S., and John L. Batchelor. *The Illustrated History of Seaplanes and Flying Boats*. London: Hamlyn [etc.], 1980.

Casey, Louis S. *Curtiss, the Hammondsport Era, 1907-1915*. New York: Crown Publishers, 1981.

Cobianchi, Mario. *Pionieri dell'aviazione in Italia, con rare e storiche illustrazioni*. Roma: Editoriale Aeronautica, 1943.

Coletta, Paolo Enrico. *Patrick N.L. Bellinger and U.S. Naval Aviation*. Lanham, Md: University Press of America, 1987.

Coletta, Paolo Enrico. *Patrick N.L. Bellinger and U.S. Naval Aviation*. Lanham, Md: University Press of America, 1987.

Curtiss Aeroplane Co., Hammondsport, N.Y. *Curtiss Aeroplanes*. Hammondsport, N.Y.: The Company, 1912.

Curtiss Aeroplane and Motor Corporation. *The Curtiss Standard Model OX Aeronautical Motor Hand Book*. Buffalo: Issued by Curtiss Aeroplane and Motor Corporation, 1918.

Curtiss, Glenn Hammond, and Augustus Post. *The Curtiss Aviation Book*. New York: Frederick A. Stokes Company, 1912.

Dyke, A. L. *Dyke's Automobile and Gasoline Engine Encyclopedia; The Elementary Principles, Construction, Operation and Repair of Automobiles, Gasoline Engines and Automobile Electric Systems; Including Trucks, Tractors, and Motorcycles, Simple, Thorough and Practical*. Chicago: Goodheart-Willcox Co, 1922.

—. *Dyke's Aircraft Engine Instructor. Third-Run with Additions*. Chicago: Goodheart-Willcox Co, 1929.

Ellis, Frank H. *Canada's Flying Heritage*. [Toronto]: University of Toronto Press, 1980.

Fresh, J. Norman, and Richard D. Murphy. *Commemorative Reports on the A-1 Hydroaeroplane for the Golden Anniversary of Naval Aviation*. Ft. Belvoir: Defense Technical Information Center, 1961.

Gordon, William Reed. *Keuka Lake Memories; The Champagne Country*. 1967.

Grigoryev, A. B. *Albatrosy. Iz istorii gidroaviatsii*. Moscow: Mashinostroyeniye, 1989.

Grossnick, Roy A., and William J. Armstrong. *United States Naval Aviation, 1910-1995*. Washington, D.C.: Naval Historical Center, Dept. of the Navy, 1997.

Gsell, Robert, and Werner Krebser. *25 jahre luftkutscher; vom luftsprung zur luftbeherrschung, mit 32 bildern*. Erlenbach: E. Rentsch, 1936.

Hatch, Alden. *Glenn Curtiss, Pioneer of Naval Aviation*. New York: J. Messner, inc, 1942.

Hatfield, D. D. *Aeroplane (or Flying Machine) Scrap Book: Amazing Developments in American Aeronautics, 1911-1929*. [Inglewood, Calif.]: Alumni Library, Northrop Institute of Technology, 1971.

Hayward, Charles B. *Practical Aeronautics; An Understandable Presentation of Interesting and Essential Facts in Aeronautical Science*. Chicago: American school of correspondence, 1912.

Horgan, James J. *City of Flight: The History of Aviation in St. Louis*. Gerald, Mo: Patrice Press, 1984.

House, Kirk W. *Hell-Rider to King of the Air: Glenn Curtiss's Life of Innovation*. Warrendale, Pa: SAE International, 2003.

Jablonski, Edward. *Seawings; The Romance of the Flying Boats*. Garden City, N.Y.: Doubleday, 1972.

Knott, Richard C. *A Heritage of Wings: An Illustrated History of Navy Aviation*. Annapolis, Md: Naval Institute Press, 1997.

Kori, Katsu. *Aireview's The Fifty Years of Japanese Aviation, 1910-1960: A Picture History with 910 Photographs*. Tokyo: Kantosha Co, 1961.

Layman, R. D. *Before the Aircraft Carrier: The Development of Aviation Vessels, 1849-1922*. Annapolis, Md: Naval Institute Press, 1989.

—. *Naval Aviation in the First World War: Its Impact and Influence*. Annapolis, Md: Naval Institute Press, 1996.

Mikesh, Robert C. & Abe, Shorzoe. *Japanese aircraft 1910-1941*. London: Putnam, 1990.

Miller, Harold B. *Navy Wings*. New York: Dodd, Mead & Co, 1942.

Mitchell, Charles R., and Kirk W. House. *Glenn H. Curtiss, Aviation Pioneer*. Images of America. Charleston, SC: Arcadia, 2001.

Morton, John Fass. *Mustin: A Naval Family of the Twentieth Century*. Annapolis, Md: Naval Institute Press, 2003.

Nozawa, Tadashi. *Encyclopedia of Japanese Aircraft 1910-1945, Volume 2 Aichi, Kugisho*. Tokyo: Shupan-Kiodo, 1959.

—. *Encyclopedia of Japanese Aircraft 1910-1945, Volume 6 Import Aircraft*. Tokyo: Shupan-Kiodo, 1972.

Page, Victor Wilfred. *Modern Aviation Engines: Design, Construction, Operation and Repair*. New York: Henley, 1929.

Peattie, Mark R. *Sunburst: The Rise of Japanese Naval Air Power, 1909-1941*. Annapolis, Md: Naval Institute Press, 2001.

Reynolds, Clark G. *Admiral John H. Towers: The Struggle for Naval Air Supremacy*. Annapolis, Md: Naval Institute Press, 1991.

Richardson, H.C. *Hydromechanic Experiments with Flying Boat Hulls*. Smithsonian miscellaneous collections, vol 62, nr. 2. Washington: Smithsonian Institution, 1914.

Rinek, Larry M. *Glenn H. Curtiss: An Early American Innovator in Aviation and Motorcycle Engines*. SAE technical paper series, 940571. Warrendale, PA: SAE Historical Committee, 1994.

Rivière, Pierre. *Pierre Rivière. Les Hydro-aéroplanes*. Paris: Libr. aéronaut, 1912.

Roseberry, Cecil R. 1972. *Glenn Curtiss: pioneer of flight*. Garden City, N.Y.: Doubleday.

Rösner, Karl F. M. *Das Flugzeug für die Kriegsmarine und den Wassersport; Theorie und Praxis im Bau der Wasserflugzeuge (und gleitboote)*. Berlin-Charlottenburg: C.J.E. Volckmann nachf. G.M.B.H., 1912.

Scharff, Robert, and Walter S. Taylor. *Over Land and Sea; A Biography of Glenn Hammond Curtiss*. New York: D. McKay Co, 1968.

Seely, Lyman J. *Flying Pioneers at Hammondsport, New York. A Very Brief Outline of the History of "The Cradle of Aviation" and of the Work of Invention, Development and Demonstration of Aeroplanes Done There by Glenn H. Curtiss, Alexander Graham Bell, the Aerial Experiment Association and Their Associates between 1908-14*. Auburn, N.Y.: Fenton Press], 1929.

Shirley, Noel C. *United States Naval Aviation 1910-1918*. Schiffer military history. Atglen, PA: Schiffer Pub, 2000.

Studer, Clara. *Sky Storming Yankee; the Life of Glenn Curtiss*. Literature and history of aviation. [New York]: Arno Press, 1972.

Swanborough, Gordon, and Peter M. Bowers. *United States Navy Aircraft Since 1911*. New York: Funk & Wagnalls, 1968.

Tily, James C. *The Uniforms of the United States Navy*. New York: T. Yoseloff, 1964.

Treadwell, Terry C. *The First Naval Air War*. Stroud: Tempus, 2002.

Turnbull, Archibald Douglas, and Clifford Lee Lord. *History of United States Naval Aviation*. New Haven: Yale University Press, 1949.

United States. *Annual Reports of the Navy Department for the Fiscal Year 1910*. Washington: U.S. G.P.O. 1910.

United States. *Annual Reports of the Navy Department for the Fiscal Year 1911*. Washington: U.S. G.P.O. 1912.

United States. *Annual Reports of the Navy Department for the Fiscal Year 1912*. Washington: U.S. G.P.O. 1913.

United States. *Annual Reports of the Navy Department for the Fiscal Year 1913*. Washington: U.S. G.P.O. 1914.

United States. *Aviation Log Curtiss Hydroaeroplane Navy No. A-1: 1 July 1911 to 16 October 1912*. United States: Navy Dept, 1911.

United States. *Aviation Log Curtiss Hydroaeroplane Navy No. AX-1: A-2 Converted to E-1, September 1913, Rebuilt December 1913, Renumbered March 1914*. United States: Navy Dept, 1914.

Van Deurs, George. *Anchors in the Sky: Spuds Ellyson, the First Naval Aviator*. San Rafael, Calif: Presidio Press, 1978.

—. *Wings for the Fleet; A Narrative of Naval Aviation's Early Development, 1910-1916*. Annapolis: U.S. Naval Institute, 1966.

Vergara, George L. *Hugh Robinson, Pioneer Aviator*. Gainesville: University Press of Florida, 1995.

Verrill, A. Hyatt. *Harper's Aircraft Book; Why Aeroplanes Fly, How to Make Models, and All About Aircraft, Little and Big*. Harper's practical books for boys. New York: Harper & Bros, 1913.

Waterman, Waldo Dean, and Jack Carpenter. *Waldo, Pioneer Aviator: A Personal History of American Aviation, 1910-1944*. Carlisle, Mass., U.S.A.: Arsdalen, Bosch, 1988.

Wiley, Frank W. *Montana and the Sky; The Beginning of Aviation in the Land of the Shining Mountains.* [Helena]: Montana Aeronautics Commission, 1966.

Woodhouse, Henry. *Textbook of Naval Aeronautics.* New York: The Century Co, 1917.

Periodicals Reading List

Aerial Age Weekly. 1915. New York City: Aerial Age Co.

Aero Club of America Bulletin. New York: The Club.

Aeronautics (New York : 1909 -1915). 1900s. New York: Aeronautics Press.

Aero and Hydro; America's Aviation Weekly. Chicago, etc: Noel & Company, etc.

American Aviation Historical Society Journal. Santa Ana, Calif. [etc.]: American Aviation Historical Society.

Cross & Cockade Journal. Santa Ana, Calif: Cross & Cockade, the Society of World War I Aero Historians.

Curtiss Flyleaf. Buffalo, N.Y.: Public and Internal Relations Dept. of Curtiss-Wright Corp., Airplane Division.

Flying. New York, N.Y.: Published by the Flying Association at the Office of the Aero Club of America.

La Navigazione Aerea: Rivista Italiana d'aeronautica. 1912. Rome: Casa Editrice Enrico Voghera.

Over the Front. Dallas, Texas: League of World War I Aviation Historians.

Proceedings. U.S. Naval Institute.

Scientific American. Supplement. 1911. New York: Munn and Co., etc.

Tekhnika vozdukhoplavaniia: Ezhemesiuchnyi nauchno-tekhnicheskii zhurnal izdavaemyi VII vozdukhoplavatelnym otdelom Imperatorskago Russkago Technich. Obshchestva. S-Peterburg: Imperatorskoe Russkoe tekhn. obshchestvo. Naidenov, V. F., & Vorobev, V. N. (1912-13).

Windsock International. 1985. Berkhamsted, Hertfordshire: Albatross Productions, Ltd.

W.W.1 Aero. Poughkeepsie, NY: World War 1 Aeroplanes, Inc.

Sources of Archival Information

Glenn H. Curtiss Museum, Hammondsport, New York

Linda Hall Library, Kansas City, Missouri

Montana Historical Society, Helena, Montana

Musée de l'Air et de l'Espace, Paris, France

Museum of Flight, Seattle, Washington

Museum of History and Industry, Seattle, Washington

National Air and Space Museum, Washington, D.C.

National Naval Aviation Museum, Pensacola, Florida

Naval History Center, Photographic Section, Washington, D.C.

San Diego Air & Space Museum, San Diego, California

San Diego Historical Society, San Diego, California

Seattle Public Library, Seattle, Washington

U.S. Naval Institute, Annapolis, Maryland

University of Southern California, Los Angeles

University of Texas-Dallas, Dallas Texas

Western Reserve Historical Society, Cleveland, Ohio

Wisconsin Historical Society, Madison, Wisconsin

Wright State University Libraries, Dayton, Ohio

Name Index

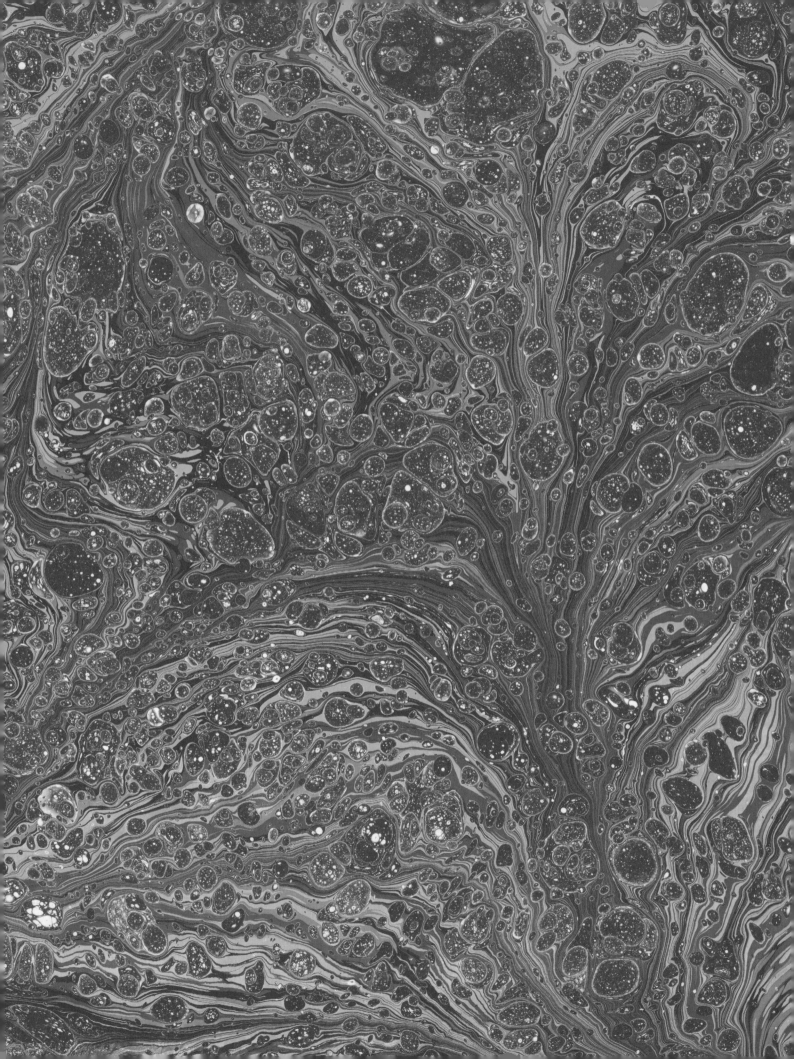